MW00533741

How to Share Christ

with Your Friends of Another Faith

Dr. Jeff Brawner

HANNIBAL BOOKS
www.hannibalbooks.com

Copyright Jeff Brawner, 2012
All Rights Reserved.

Printed in the United States of America
by Versa Press
Cover design by Debbie King

Unless otherwise indicated
all Scriptures taken from the *New King James Version*.
Copyright 1979, 1980, 1982 by Thomas Nelson, Inc. Used by
permission. All rights reserved.
Library of Congress Control Number: 201294400
ISBN 978-1-61315-024-5

Hannibal Books
313 South 11th Street, Suite A
Garland, TX 75040
1-800-747-0738
hannibalbooks@earthlink.net

Dedicated

to my wife, **Christy,**
who for 18 years has stood by me;

my daughters, **Anna and Lizzy**, who have brought
immeasurable joy to my life;

and the **countless nameless individuals** who, in obscurity,
minister for the Father. With little to no fanfare
they share their faith with their friends.

And of course, I dedicate this book to
my **Lord and Savior, Jesus Christ**.

What others are saying about this book:

Profound, penetrating, and *practical* are words that spring to mind when describing this extremely original book on evangelizing all peoples. Jeff Brawner combines a scholar's grasp of theology with a missionary's heart for the lost to produce one of the finest works in years on evangelism.

Dr. Robin Hadaway, interim president and professor of missions
Midwestern Baptist Theological Seminary, Kansas City, MO

One could not praise this book too much! Jeff Brawner has produced the most thorough, informative, and practical publication on evangelizing world religions that I have ever read. This book is a "step-by-step" manual for every Christian who is serious about fulfilling the Great Commission locally and throughout the world.

Dr. Archie Mason, senior pastor
Central Baptist Church, Central Campus/Journey Campus, Jonesboro, AR

In his new book Jeff Brawner has presented an outstanding introduction to biblical evangelism. More than producing just an exercise in theory, Dr. Brawner has written a practical guide for every believer to use in sharing his or her faith. This book covers a general approach to evangelism practice and then develops that biblical model for a number of different sects and religions. The included guides are clear and concise; the material will benefit the new or experienced believer. I give this book my highest recommendation.

Dr. Michael Spradlin, president
Mid-America Baptist Theological Seminary, Cordova, TN

Jeff Brawner has done an incredible job of encouraging believers to be "salt and light" to people—especially to those of other faiths—who do not know Christ. This practical approach is a must-read for all Christians who have a heart for the lost of our world."

Steve Marcum, minister, missions
Bellevue Baptist Church, Cordova, TN

4

Knowing how to be accepting of other people and to avoid social gaffes in today's multi-cultural society is not enough; we are called to be witnesses for Christ to those who live around us. This book is an excellent resource for those who have heard their share of admonitions to witness to people of other religions and ask the question, "But where do I start?" This book is a carefully written and well-organized manual for people who seek a way to spread the Good News to those who may have appeared unreachable to them. I recommend it for individual reading or group study.

Dr. Winfried Corduan, author
Neighboring Faiths and *Pocket Guide to World Religions*

<u>TO CONTACT THE AUTHOR</u>
<u>WRITE TO HIM AT</u>

jbrawner@mabts.edu

To get updates and visit with Jeff Brawner on Facebook,
type in the book's title,
How to Share Christ with Your Friends of Another Faith,
in Facebook's search engine.

Acknowledgements

For years I have wanted to write a book on world religions. I didn't want the book to be theoretical, however. I wanted it to be a practical, step-by-step vehicle. I never began to write because I didn't feel capable of addressing all the variety of religions. Mercifully, the Lord moved me to realize that I didn't have all the answers; in fact, no one does. However, in the midst of my limited knowledge, I have been blessed to be surrounded by people who for years have been hands-on in areas of the world that I have not had the privilege of serving.

None of these individuals is famous. They are all just diligent servants of the King of Kings. First, I'd like to thank all of the people that contributed to this book. They worked for free and gave their time abundantly. The 15 that shared their evangelistic techniques not only are personal friends, they are committed evangelists for Christ. I am deeply indebted.

A hearty thanks to my missions professors at Mid-America Baptist Seminary—Dr. Stan May and Dr. Steve Wilkes—who helped strengthen my love for a lost world. Thank you to Dr. Winfried Corduan, who took time to proof this work to make sure I hadn't made any profound errors. To the men and women that I have served beside long-term in both America and Brazil as a pastor and a missionary, to this day your fervor has helped to keep me in the fight. To my mom, an English teacher for 28 years, thanks for the help with the grammar. I commit to learning how to use a comma—someday.

My wife, Christy, is an equally important proofreader. To her and our two daughters, Anna and Lizzy—thanks not only for your input but also your love. To the God-fearing men and women who helped lead me to Christ—Mom and Dad, Bobby and Dr. Jim Shaw, Dr. Don Dunavant, and the nameless speaker at JoyExplo 1989—thank you for caring enough about my soul to share Christ with me.

Finally and most importantly, I again acknowledge my Lord and Savior Jesus Christ. I owe Him . . . everything.

Contents

Foreword

Dr. Jeff Brawner is both an academic and a practitioner. He is a man who does not just talk the talk but also walks the walk. He is one professor of missions who stays on the front lines of the battle and not just in the classroom. He knows the theory, but he knows better how to put it all into practice in real life. Having served as a pastor and an international missionary, both from study and personal experience he knows of which he speaks.

This book is a practical "how-to" manual. If you want to know how actually to witness and to share your faith with Muslims, atheists, Buddhists, Mormons, Catholics, Protestants, and Hindus, then this book is a must-read. Not only will you find yourself reading it, you also will find yourself studying it. Not only will you find yourself studying it, but you will be applying in real life what you learn. Now, that is the kind of book I truly like—a book in which I learn both theory and also how to put it all into practice.

If you are serious about being equipped in sharing your faith cross-culturally with others from different backgrounds and religions, then this book is an absolute necessity for you. I encourage you to read it, study it, and put it to work for you.

Dr. Thomas Wade Akins
Missionary, Pioneer Missions
Author: *Sharing Your Faith with Muslims* and
    Be a 24/7 Christian

Chapter 1

Why Share Your Faith?

*Jesus said to him, "I am the way, the truth, and the life.
No one comes to the Father except through Me"*
(John 14:6).

No matter how "open-minded" and inclusive my culture tells
me to be, I just can't get around John 14:6. My bet is that most
sincere believers, deep in their hearts, can't get around this verse
either. I'm not sure Christ could have stated His case more
clearly. He is the *"way"* to the Father. No other *"way"* is avail-
able, no matter how fervently one practices his or her beliefs.

• What if someone sincerely worships a Hindu god? In
John 14:6 *sincerity*, while admirable, never is mentioned.
• What if someone fervently follows the five pillars of
Islam? In this verse *obedience*, while difficult and hon-
orable, isn't mentioned either.
• What if you take away all desire and reach Nirvana as
Buddhism teaches? In this verse *self-control*, while fruit-
ful, also is not discussed.

Truly the beginning and the end of this verse have a common
theme—Jesus. John 14:6 starts with "*I*" and ends with "*Me*". If I
start and end a proclamation about myself, I border on being nar-
cissistic. However, when Christ refers to Himself, no ego is involved. He simply is stating a fact, or as this verse references,
He is stating Truth. Christ is the only One in all eternity Who is

13

worthy to speak of self as the Solution to our problems.

The exclusivity of Christ threatens commonly held notions we have in the United States. For example, our government runs on pluralistic ideals. We are a hodgepodge of diverse people with different ideas—people who join together to hammer out compromise for the good of all. Our government, the representative body of our nation, runs on this principle. Pluralism starts in the government and filters down into all aspects of life. Just as most Americans, when asked, will claim to avoid being on the fringes politically, they also want to be viewed as open-minded and compromising in all aspects of life—even in their religion.

However, Christ's dictates do not function in the same manner. When you and I get together on the political stage, regardless of education, creed, economic conditions, or ethnicity, we are peers. We must hammer out compromise, because none of us ultimately has all the answers. Christ, with His proclamations, works differently. Christ knows what is best—in all situations, at all times. He doesn't need to compromise what He says, because our input does not balance His. He knows best. The best is . . . Him.

Consequently, Jesus has stated that the plan for our salvation is only through Him. In a world of compromise this is an uncompromising position. If we want to be popular in all social circles, we cannot hold to this truth. Christ already warns us when He states, "*In the world you will have tribulation . . .*" (John 16:33). Holding to Christ's exclusivity will be a position that costs us.

However, if what Christ states holds true, then you face a dilemma. By definition the only way to salvation is through Christ, but many of those moral, honorable people around you do not follow Christ. Many of them follow another "divine" entity. Other friends may pay lip-service to Christ, but by the fruit of their lives they exhibit no true life change. Other friends even might be NICER than a lot of Christians you know but are doctrinally incorrect about Christ. Your dilemma quickly becomes evident. Do you believe what Christ states about Himself? If so, do you actually care enough about your friend/acquaintance or co-worker to risk sharing your faith with him or her?

If our neighbors who are Muslims, Hindus, animists, Buddhists, Mormons, Catholics, Protestants, or atheists have not given their lives to Jesus Christ as Lord and Savior, they do not have salvation.[1] How moral, how pleasant, or what kind of solid citizens they are doesn't matter. To fit into His plan they must surrender their lives to Christ.

This book is designed to help you share your exclusive faith in Christ. Your faith did not start with you, nor does it end with you. Your faith is about Jesus. You can share only what He commands you to share. And He certainly commands you to share:

> *"Go therefore and make disciples of all nations, baptizing them in the name of the Father and of the Son and of the Holy Spirit, teaching them to observe all things that I have commanded you . . ."* (Mt. 28:19-20a).

> *And He said to them, "Go into all the world and preach the gospel to every creature"* (Mark 16:15).

> *"But you shall receive power when the Holy Spirit has come upon you; and you shall be witnesses to Me in Jerusalem, and in all Judea and Samaria, and to the end of the earth"* (Acts 1:8b).

Christ's message is readily apparent. Jesus always intended for His disciples to go into the entire world—among all peoples—and share HIM. You and I are to do the same.

This book was written to show you how to follow Christ's command about sharing your faith. This book is purposely designed to be different from any other book on evangelism/world religions. The book assumes the following:

- You have an inward desire to share Christ with someone of a different faith but don't know how.
- You are not looking for a treatise on every religion in the world. You need a brief summary of your friend's religion so you can work with him or her.
- You need a STEP-BY-STEP plan in sharing your faith — a guide telling you exactly what to say from the moment you walk in the door until the time you might lead someone to pray to give his or her life to Christ.
- You lead a busy life. Time for pleasure-reading is a luxury you do not have. Consequently, the chapter on your religion of interest needs to be brief. You might not even have time to read this entire book. In fact, the book needs to be designed so that as you witness, you can read only the chapter about your friend's particular belief system and do fine. You want this book to be as simple and hands-on as possible.

I think these four assumptions express the situation of many believers in Christ. After 16 years in the ministry as a youth minister, then a missionary, then a pastor, and now a professor at a seminary, I have observed that many good books about world religions have been written by very godly individuals. I strongly suggest supplementing this book with some of the titles listed at the conclusion of my book. However, I also have noted that when the time arrives for you to really describe how to share your faith, most books become disappointingly vague.

One of my mentors in the ministry once told me, "Most people have a difficult time going from the theoretical to the practical. You MUST make ministry practical." I believe he's right.

Most people do not need general ideas about how to share their faith. They need a specific step-by-step plan. In light of this fact each chapter of the book will have three parts. Each chapter gives—

1) A brief overview of a particular belief system (religion).

2) A detailed summary of a plan(s) to witness to the individual. The plan will detail all necessary steps to a gospel witness. It will show how to start a conversation, how to find a bridge in conversation to the gospel, and how to use specific verses while you share the gospel. The idea of this section is to show you a STEP-BY-STEP conversation. Obviously you don't have to follow these plans exactly, but this book gives you patterns to follow.

3) Questions an adherent to that faith might ask you.

I hope this book will give you a beginning step in the process of sharing your faith with someone involved in a religion or belief system. My prayer is that you will see your friend arrive at the point of accepting a saving faith in the Lord Jesus Christ.

Second Peter 3:9 says, *The Lord is not slow in keeping his promise, as some understand slowness. Instead he is patient with you, not wanting anyone to perish, but everyone to come to repentance* (NIV).

As believers, we often toil to learn God's will for our lives. The truth is, we can KNOW one aspect of God's will. He longs for your friend to repent. Sharing your faith most certainly will fall within His will.

In closing, some words of caution:

First, no presentation of the plan of salvation is guaranteed to provide success. If someone had designed the perfect approach to witness to Muslims or Hindus—a method that always brings someone to salvation—his or her plan by now would be a best-seller. We would have seen, in mass, Muslims or Hindus trust Christ. No evangelistic techniques in this world guarantee salvation. Why not? Maybe the Lord knows that if He gives us a step-by-step plan that guarantees that someone will trust Christ every time a person hears it, then we would start putting our trust in the plan rather than in Him. Just share your faith. The results are up to Him.

Second, always use the plans given here as a base, but adapt as you become more confident. We are trying to give you a practical step-by-step guide. The book contains plans that you can follow. However, do not become bondservants to these plans. As time progresses, make these plans your own. For example, change this book's suggested bridges to the gospel and suggested illustrations to fit your individual scenario. Jesus modified His approaches to fit the situation. He approached the gospel in radically different ways—whether He spoke to the woman at the well (John 4), a blind man (John 10) or Matthew (Mt. 9). He always found ways to personalize the message to the hearer.

Although I have written this book in a manner in which you can read only the chapter that pertains to your individual friend, I encourage you to read through the chapter either on Roman Catholicism or (Nominal) Protestantism. In those chapters I give a very detailed outline of how to utilize five verses from the book of Romans. Each of these chapters contains such detail that if you become nervous about what to say as you witness, to complete the witness you actually could just READ those sections to your friend. However, these five verses actually explain the gospel in a way that you can use for all chapters in this book. If you want a thorough review of how to share the gospel message itself, you would be wise to take five minutes and read those sections regardless of what religion on which you are focusing.

Third, don't change the final message. You can change the bridges, illustrations, and even verses that you might use. However, the gospel DOES NOT CHANGE. What is the *gospel*? The Bible gives a simple answer. 1 Corinthians 15:1-4 (NIV) says,

Now, brothers, I want to remind you of the gospel I preached to you, which you received and on which you have taken your stand. By this gospel you are saved, if you hold firmly to the word I preached to you. Otherwise, you have believed in vain. For what I received I passed on to you as of first importance that Christ died for our sins according to the Scriptures, that he was buried, that he was raised on the third day according to the Scriptures.

What is the *gospel*? The gospel simply is that Jesus died, was buried, and three days later rose from the grave for our sins. You never change that part of the message. That part of the message is not part of a technique. Instead it reflects the core truth in all the universe.

Fourth, don't preach; just share. Leave the preaching to the preachers. Be the concerned friend who, in love, is sharing the best news you've ever received. I'm a preacher. When I hear a preacher using his "preaching voice" off the stage (and oftentimes on it), I just cringe. Imagine how people in a lost world feel when they hear someone move from "speaking to them" to "preaching at them".

Fifth, Scripture says that today is the *day of salvation* (2 Cor. 6:2). Anyone can get saved at any time. However, the Bible doesn't say that you must bring your friend to salvation today. Don't be afraid to take your time. Share your faith with boldness. If your friend is not ready, that's OK. Let the Holy Spirit move you to stop or proceed as He sees fit.

Sixth, someone once told me that the joy of working among a harvest is not how many people trust Christ but how many people give you a chance to share with them. It's the OPENNESS of people that defines a harvest. Will someone make a decision to follow Christ every time you follow these steps? I hope so! However, realistically, this will not be the case. Instead remember that part of the glory of sharing your faith is the joy that obedience brings in your life. Witnessing brings you the realization that you were obedient to God and that because of your obedience He will reveal Himself in ways you never could have imagined.

Seventh, form the habit of keeping a Bible in your car, pocket, or purse. You never, ever know when an opportunity to share your faith will arise. I love being able to share my testimony. Telling what Christ has done for me is powerful. However, nothing replaces being able to point to specific verses that apply to an individual's life. Visually you can show your friend that the authority of your life isn't your experience but is the Word of God.

Eighth, and finally, don't be afraid to say, "I don't know, but I'll get back to you after I find the answer." You cannot imagine how a humble response works in a Western culture. This book hopefully provides an example. Do I feel as though I am an expert in witnessing to all of these religions? No. Do I have experience with all of them? Yes. However, when I wrote this book, I realized I had colleagues that knew more about witnessing to Muslim, Buddhists, and Hindus than I did, so I contacted them. Huge portions of this book are attributed to individuals who know far more than I. In like manner, you're never wrong to pause and say to your friend, "I need to ask someone else about that issue." This takes the pressure off you and off the person to whom you're witnessing as well. The person will respect you for your transparency. No one likes a "know-it-all".

God bless you for taking the time to read this book. You can read it in its entirety or skip to the chapter that deals with your friend specifically.

---

[1]A reader might ask, "What about other religions, such as Judaism, Taoism, Scientology, that are not specifically addressed in this book?" Obviously adherents to those faiths need Christ and are infinitely valuable before the Lord. Many of the general principles we have taught in this book will work with those groups as well. Hopefully, future editions of the book can expand to a variety of other faiths.

Chapter 2

What if I Don't Have Friends from Another Religious Background?

If you think that overnight, the world around you hasn't become multi-cultural, think again. A few months ago the services of the church my wife and I attend didn't meet one Sunday night. We stopped at a local mall in Memphis, TN, and were overwhelmed at what we saw. Memphis, while certainly not a "churched" city, does have a lot of strong Christians and capable churches. The majority of those churches contain two ethnic groups—Caucasian and/or African American.

However, as I walked into the food court of the mall, I was surprised and amazed. Whereas the number of middle-class white and African-Americans was small, a potpourri of nationalities was represented. The mall, surrounded by strong, middle-class churches, was filled with all the ethnic groups that did NOT have strong churches for them. Latinos, Arabs, Persians, Eastern Europeans, and Africans all were represented. I began to be under great conviction. Where is the church community for these folks? Who is reaching out to the smaller ethnic groups in Memphis?

I guarantee you that if you live in just about any size municipality in America now, you have individuals from all over the world in your town. What if you are in a small town? Millions of South Americans are living in rural farming communities; you can befriend these persons. In large cities, the day of having predominantly white or black neighborhoods rapidly is vanishing. On my street Germans live two doors down, Mexicans live across the street, African-Americans are at the end of the cove, and a few Caucasian transplants from around the country are nearby. I guarantee you—the day of homogeneity in whatever town you live is over.[1]

Being of a different ethnicity does not mean one is non-Christian, however. Caucasians and African-Americans do not have the corner on being born-again believers. Millions of Latinos, Africans, and Asians are fervent followers of our Lord. Many of these have shown their love for Christ under far more difficult circumstances than those of us in the American church have.

However, God is bringing to our doorstep people from a multitude of nationalities and a multitude of religions. The immense numbers of adherents of other religions in the United States is staggering.[2] In a sense, the plurality of the religious world has arrived here. If you don't have an acquaintance of another religion, then pause, look around, and see the opportunities that God has placed before you. God might be calling you to reach out and make a new friend.

How to Make Friends with Someone of a Different Nationality or Religion

Jesus was sent to earth "*to seek and to save that which was lost*" (Luke 19:10). How does one *seek* out those who are lost? This brief chapter gives you important ideas of how to find people who do not know Christ. Why should you do this? Because eventually if you get in the habit of forming friends from outside your typical circle, opportunities to share your faith will multiply.

Most believers have one major reason why they don't witness to people. What is that problem? They don't really know any lost people. They know *of* them, but they don't have any true relationships with lost people. How can you bridge that gap and make relationships with lost people? Below are some simple steps that I have found open doors to relationships with the unchurched world.

1) Take your mobile digital device out of your ears. I am not anti-electronic devices. I am not anti-music. However, I AM against being anti-social. I was discussing with a friend of mine about working out at the gym and how it's such a wonderful place to meet people. He sheepishly admitted, "The truth is, I don't want to meet people. I just want to put my iPod® in and zone out after work."

Yes, occasionally "zoning out" is pleasant, but we have gone to the extreme of zoning out whenever we aren't at work, school, or church. If your device is in your ear, how are you going to socially interact with the lost world? Conversations don't start with plugs in your ear. If you follow this step, you will be amazed at how many more conversations you have with folks.

2) Change your place of business. A few years ago a group of women opened a hair salon close to my house. I'm far more comfortable going to a barber shop full of guys. However, this shop was owned by a group of Indians. They were thorough, friendly, less expensive, and yes . . . not Christians. I have had the opportunity to discuss Christianity with them. Granted, a gender barrier inhibited how far I could pursue a friendship relationship. Consequently, I mentioned to a group of woman from my church that this salon did a good job on hair and nails. (No, they had not done my nails; I had to make an assumption on that one.) Some woman in the church started to frequent the salon as well; PRESTO! an immediate interaction occurred between middle-class, Caucasian Christians and middle-class Indian Hindus.

3) Join a gym. I can be brief on this one. I never have led anyone in a sinner's prayer in the middle of my gym. No one who sees me in shorts and a no-sleeve shirt wants to get TOO close to me. Having said that, as I sat down to write this chapter, I was amazed at how many new people I've met and with whom I've conversed during the past few weeks since I began spending time at the gym. Among them are ex-pro baseball player, a Presbyterian army chaplain, and a computer engineer from the Ukraine. How often would I have run into those guys if I merely had been watching TV at my house? Never. Go join a gym. If you live in a big city, your options of meeting people after work are limited anyway. Plus, most of us could stand to lose 15 pounds.

4) Bake a cake. OK, I can't bake anything. However, I can be aware when someone new moves into my neighborhood. Today most people have lost the art of greeting newcomers in a neighborhood. Keep your eyes open; when people move in, take them a housewarming gift. Will it guarantee you a witnessing opportunity? No. However, in most cases this act of kindness engenders friendship immediately. Plus, it might lead to a witness later. By the way, if you want to do this on a larger scale, your local church can go to one of many companies that provide addresses of newcomers in a particular zip code. Have a standard church policy to deliver to each new home a bag of cookies or some housewarming gift. You'll hit people from all walks of life.

5) Take an international neighbor or colleague to the grocery store. As a professor at a school which has many students from around the world, I constantly am reminded of a sad truth. When people arrive in America from other countries, EVERYTHING is complicated. These people want to know: Where does one buy food? How does someone pay bills? Where does one call if trouble occurs?

These tasks which most of us take for granted almost can be insurmountable to an international person who just arrives in town. Why don't you solve one or more of those problems by just donating an hour of your time? If you know of a new international in town, why don't you offer to take him or her to the grocery store? Many probably could use the ride; your expertise in how much things should cost can be invaluable to that newcomer. Last week a Congolese man that I am getting to know was riding his bicycle up a busy road. I pulled over and asked where he was going. He was going to ride another mile up the road in the hopes of finding a place that could make copies of a paper. He had no idea where to go for this service, but he was determined to get this task done. I threw his bike in the back of the car and drove to a place to get copies. This task didn't take 15 minutes of my time, but in the process I gained a friend.

6) Hang out with your friends on Sunday, but intentionally spend much of your time with a lost world. As the years go by, Evangelicals become more and more isolated. Church functions, ministries, sports events, worship services . . . the lists of activities goes on and on. Ultimately, take some time to spend with your Christian friends. However, during the week, if you've got a free lunch break, sit down with someone who evidently is sitting alone. I'll never forget that one of the prettiest cheerleaders at the college I attended never ate with the "cool" kids. She always took time to eat with the international students who were trying to fit in. Her testimony still speaks to me today. How often and for how long do you attempt to sit down with the lonely, the down-and- out, or the stranger?

7) Learn a language. You may be thinking, "He's got to be kidding!" Well, not really, but please read to the end of this section before you completely discount this idea.

Some readers actually might be able to learn a language with ease. However, I'm well aware that for MOST of us this just isn't the case. (Anyone remember high-school Spanish or French and how inept you felt?)

However, you CAN learn a language or at least have a working knowledge of one. As a missionary I learned a truth on the mission field: EVERY missionary ends up learning the language. We all have the mental faculties to learn another language. However, if you have neither the time nor the inclination to learn another language, you certainly can pick up a few phrases. Why?

Missionaries learn languages not only to share their faith but also to build friendships. You cannot imagine how excited people become when you converse in their language. They are honored that you believe that their language is important to learn. After all, most everyone wants to learn English; they will be curious as to why you are attempting to learn their language.

In light of this fact try to learn just a few phrases in the language of someone you are beginning to try to get to know better. You can learn phrases such as "How are you?", "You look nice today", "Hello", and "Goodbye". Simple phrases such as these, that anyone can learn, can be a nice second step in bridging the divide between someone you already know on a surface level and someone with whom you would like to garner a deeper relationship.

8) Forget yourself. Last but not least, much of the time we don't have our eyes open to people to whom we could minister because we are too busy thinking about our own needs. Ever stopped to *really* listen to conversations? (Yes, I do mean eavesdrop!) They typically are filled with self-involved topics. If you constantly are thinking about yourself, your errands, your children, your entertainment, and your priorities, you are not taking time to open your eyes and to see other people's needs. Many people do not have a sufficient number of friends/contacts because they don't put sufficient time and mental energy into trying to make friends. We never, ever, ever have a shortage of lonely Buddhists, Muslims, Catholics, and Protestants around us. This world is hurting. I've become convinced we have become so self-involved, we cannot even see the brokenness around us.

This is not an exhaustive list. These simply represent ideas to help you make friends. I hope that if you incorporate these eight ideas, more opportunities to make friends will present themselves. In a world in which most folks are walking around feeling completely alone, Christians never will find themselves without someone with whom to minister.

[1]Census data shows that the United States is 72.4 percent white and 12.6 percent black. If 16 percent of the population is of another ethnicity and the population of the U.S. in 2012 roughly was 310 million, 49.6 million people are of another ethnicity. Source: *http://quickfacts.census, gov/qjd/states/47000.html* (accessed 11-13-2011).

[2]The 2012 Statistical Abstract produced by the U.S. Census Bureau of people who voluntarily designated a religious preference (federal law now prohibits the census from requiring someone to answer a question about religious preferences) shows the following religions' U.S. population: Buddhists, 1.189 million; Muslims, 1.34 million; Jewish, 2.68 million; Unitarian, 586,000; Hindu, 582,000.

Chapter 3

How to Witness
to Your Roman Catholic Friends

Let's first clear the obvious question out of the way. Is this book saying that all Roman Catholics need to be saved? Not at all. However, is this book saying that if a Roman Catholic trusts in Mary, in one's own works, or in obtaining salvation through the church, he or she needs to be saved? Most definitely—in the same way Protestants or Evangelicals who put their trust in their good actions or in their positions in the church ("I'm a deacon" or "I'm a tither") need to be saved. The point of salvation doesn't center on your subset of Christianity but on whether you have surrendered your life to Christ.

Avoiding discussion, however, of certain aspects of the Catholic faith that can interfere with someone truly understanding the gospel would be intellectually dishonest. Unless an Evangelical understands our differences with Rome, the person really can't openly and honestly dialogue with Catholic friends.

Overview of the Catholic Faith:
How Did the Church Get Here?

At first, no Catholic/Protestant Church existed. Only the church existed. The first 300 years of Christianity centered on both expansion and survival in the midst of persecution. In the first century, Christianity expanded rapidly. The Book of Acts tells us that the church immediately spread to places such as Tunisia, Egypt, Greece, Turkey, Israel, Iraq, and Iran. If you find believers from Southwestern India, with confidence they will tell you that in the first century, the Apostle Thomas arrived at their doorstep as well. If you go to Spain, they've even named a city after their supposed first-century church's founder (*Santiago* means St. James). In other words the church grew much farther and much faster than we typically think.

In the next two centuries the church established far more than being footholds in these areas and laid the groundwork to becoming the dominant religion of each area. By 380 A.D. the church was the official religion of the Roman Empire. By the sixth century the church dominated Europe and Africa and looked as if it would take all of the Middle East including Arabia.[1] Many scholars are fairly confident that by the seventh century the church had spread across Europe and Asia and was far more than just a Western European phenomenon. By no means did it dominate in most parts of Asia, but it was a presence.

In the midst of this expansion the church faced fierce persecution. To deal with the persecution the church began certain practices that seemed logical at the time but laid the groundwork for problems later. One example includes the idea of praying to the saints.

Martyrdom became quite prevalent in the church. Many people began to pay reverence to those who had been martyred. Quite quickly in the early church, Christians began to meet at the burial grounds of the martyrs. Relatively quickly the practice morphed from meeting at the martyr's burial grounds to asking the deceased martyrs for daily help. This helped form the practice of praying to saints. By the sixth century Pope Gregory the Great popularized praying to saints; this core aspect of the Catholic Church was secured for history.

Another example is Mariolatry. As the early church expanded, heresy became a true problem. The church had to find ways to deal with heretical ideas. Great debates formed over the divinity/humanity of Christ. Some groups tried to minimize His divinity, while others tried to minimize His humanity. At a meeting of bishops in Constantinople the leaders fought to create a creed that would deal with a certain heresy called Apollinarianism. This heresy minimized the humanity of Jesus. To deal with this heresy the church leaders began to call Mary the "Mother of God". Of course, logically speaking, God doesn't need an earthly mother. The believers, at the time, were using this terminology to show that Mary wasn't only the mother of a man but was the Mother of the Divine Christ as well. They were trying to use intelligent phrasing to combat a heresy. However, in the process they laid the groundwork for the Mary-worship that Catholics employ today.[2]

Practices such as these evolved into doctrines contrary to Scripture, but not until the 16th century did any of these issues individually bring the church to the breaking point. In the 16th century the practice of selling indulgences became very prominent in the church. Indulgences focused on making a donation to the church for the purposes of buying time out of purgatory for loved ones. This practice proved to be too much for a young monk named Martin Luther, who in 1517 nailed 95 theses on the door of a church in Wittenberg, Germany; his theses detailed the abuses of the church.

Luther never intended to split from the church—only to help reform some unbiblical practices. In the end, however, Martin Luther set off a chain of events that throughout history ultimately caused millions to break off from the Catholic Church. Throughout history was Martin Luther the only person to stand up against the abuses of the church? Most certainly not. Throughout the centuries churches have decried the abuses of the Catholic Church. However, from Luther, Calvin, Knox, Zwingli, and a group called the *Anabaptists*, many different denominations were born. All of these churches have a few common denominators. All hold to salvation through Christ alone, the preeminence of Scripture over tradition, and salvation by grace instead of works. We call these the *Protestant churches.*

Throughout the next few hundred years the dividing line between Catholics and Protestants grew quite wide. Of course, attempts have been made to try to bridge the gap between the two. However, when one looks at how the Catholic Church really teaches one must be saved, the differences between Catholics and Protestants become evident. For a Catholic to be saved, one must be part of the Catholic Church and to varying degrees follow seven key sacraments. The seven sacraments are:

1) Baptism
2) Eucharist (the Lord's Supper)
3) Reconciliation (Penance)
4) Confirmation
5) Marriage
6) Holy Order (Ordination)
7) Anointing of the Sick (Extreme Unction)[3]

While, in truth, one is not harmed by being in a church nor participating in marriage, baptism, and the Lord's Supper, none of these acts can bring salvation to one's life. The minute a person begins to think that the church or his or her actions can save that individual, he or she has delved into a salvation based on "works". The Bible is very clear that salvation can occur only by grace through faith in Christ. No one else and nothing else can save. Ephesians 2:8-9 says, *For by grace you have been saved through faith, and that not of yourselves; it is the gift of God, not of works, lest anyone should boast.*

No educated Protestant or Evangelical would claim that all Catholics haven't put their trust in Christ. Millions and millions of Catholic believers all through history have participated in the growth of the true church. Apparently millions of Catholic believers today really don't understand the sacramental system and just have put their trust in Jesus. Yet these people are saved despite the Catholic teachings, not because of the official teachings. Most well-meaning Catholics that I have run across ultimately believe they are saved by grace AND works. Ultimately, if you are saved by anything other than the blood of Jesus Christ, you are putting your trust in a false god. If a Catholic, or any of us, is trusting in good works in our life, that false God is . . . ourselves. After all, who, if not ourselves, does the "work"?

How Do I Share my Faith with Catholics?

With Catholics you have some distinct advantages in sharing your faith. If you are witnessing to a Catholic, you both believe in many of the same ideas. Catholics believe in God, Jesus, and the Holy Spirit. Catholics believe in sin and the Holy Bible. In sharing with a Hindu or Muslim you do not have these similarities in belief as a great bridge to the gospel. So what steps do you take to share your faith?

Step 1—Befriend them.

Do not befriend Catholics for the purpose of witnessing to them. Befriend a Catholic because the person is created by God and is of infinite importance. That alone makes him or her worthy of your time and energy. Also, befriend Catholics because . . . you just want to be their friend! While I spent more than six years in Brazil, the largest Catholic country in the world, I can tell you that I made many Catholic friends. Yes, they went to a different church. However, during my time there the friendships that I made both at work and play proved invaluable.

People want to know that they are of value. Time investment is far more important than is financial investment. (On every anniversary I try to tell my wife this, but that typically falls on deaf ears!) Find ways initially to spend time with your Catholic friends. Take them out to eat. Drink coffee with them. Offer to help the person with an errand or household need. Watch a baseball game with the person. Chat about parenting challenges, which have similarities the world over. Make the person aware that you care. Why? Because you do care.

Step 2—Avoid the urge to just be their friend and never engage in a spiritual conversation.

Make sure, from the onset, that you determine that you at some point will share your faith. In light of this, after you determine that you will share your faith, slip into conversation something about God, church, or Jesus. Let your friend know that you are a spiritual person without having to say, "I am a spiritual person." You subtly are letting this person know that God is important to you. You easily can become so engrossed in maintaining a friendship that out of fear you will lose the friendship, you never get around to mentioning God. The solution to this dilemma is to mention God early in the relationship.

Step 3—Look for the spiritual clues.

This step might not happen. However, if your friend mentions God, church, Jesus, or conviction of some kind of "wrongdoing", then you already know you have an open door to start sharing your faith. Why?

Certain things occur that only God can bring us to do. For example, only God can convict us of sin (John 16:8) and draw people to Himself (John 12:32). We don't just seek God on our own (Rom. 3). When someone mentions God or sin, then I know that, at a minimum, God is working on his or her heart. After all, only God can cause us to become convicted of sin or to think about Him. This is an open door to step into what God already is accomplishing. If I hear a friend talking on any of these topics,

34

you better believe that very quickly thereafter I'll be saying, "May I share something with you (about Christ) . . .?"

Step 4—Seize the initiative even if spiritual clues do not present themselves.

Let's be honest: much of the time people do not make their spiritual needs plainly evident. In that case, at some point in the conversation you can use a list of spiritual questions. Henry Blackaby, in the popular study *Experiencing God*, gives a list of excellent lead-in questions to present the gospel. What are some approaches to broach the gospel? You can ask your friend:

- Do you want to talk about what is happening in your life?
- What do you see as the greatest challenge in your life?
- What is the most significant thing happening in your life now?
- How can I pray for you?
- Would you tell me what God is doing in your life?
- What is God bringing to the surface in your life?
- What particular burden has God given you?[4]

These are excellent questions. So let's flesh out exactly how to use them.

For example, if you and your friend are meeting over coffee and the Spirit has shown you that the time is right to share with your friend, you can say,

"Harold, can I ask you a personal question?"

If Harold says "Yes," then say,

"You and I have known each other for a while. Something is kind of important to me. Do you believe in something after this life?"

That question does not limit you to one denomination or even one religion. It's a fair question that is not too intrusive in our culture. Be prepared to let Harold talk. In fact, he might talk for a while. With Catholics you may hear some very divergent answers. Whatever they say, treat them with respect, because THEY DESERVE RESPECT.

Whether the person says "Yes" or "No" to the question, bridge the conversation with this statement:

"Harold, may I share something that really has impacted me?"

If you feel Harold get defensive, or if he indicates that he doesn't want to hear the answer, explain to Harold that you don't want to push but that something really did change your life. Tell you are open to sharing with him at any time.

If he appears to be ready to hear your answer, say the following:

"_____ years ago I gave my life to Christ. I cannot tell you how much this decision has changed everything about me. In fact, nothing about me is the same since that decision. Have you ever made a decision for God that changed everything about your life?" (ALTERNATE QUESTION: "If you were to die today, do you know for CERTAIN that you'd spend eternity in heaven?") Take a moment to let the person respond. Then you have arrived at the core question of the entire process. Ask your friend:

"May I show you from Scripture why I decided to give my life to Christ?" (Alternate response: "The Bible shows us how we can be certain that we'll spend eternity in heaven? May I show you what it says?")

If your friend says "yes", follow the next steps.

If the person says "no", thank him or her for listening, explain as a friend that you are ready to talk on this topic at any time, and then move on.

The key centers on GIVING YOUR FRIEND OPPORTUNITIES TO BE IN CONTROL. People in this generation of Americans, Brazilians, Africans, etc., do not particularly want you to force them to do anything. However, if they give permission to share, then they will have far more open ears to hear.

5) Sharing the plan of salvation in six easy steps

Now you are ready to explain from Scripture why you believe what you believe. This can be done by sharing from six very self-evident verses. In fact, the verses are so clear, you will see that they basically teach themselves.

Step 1—The Source

Take out your pocket New Testament. Tell your friend you want to show six verses from Scripture (Hint Hint—Time to start carrying a pocket New Testament.) Explain that you don't want to preach, but you just want to show from the Bible how God changed your life. Open your Bible to the book of 1 John 5:13 and read:

I write these things to you who believe in the name of the Son of God so that you may know that you have eternal life (1 John 5:13, NIV).

Explain that God actually wrote the Bible so that billions of individuals can know how they can have eternal life. The Bible is a love letter to your friend because God wants him or her to know Him. Scripture says He already knows us, but He wants us to know Him.

Step 2—The Problem

Turn in the Bible to Romans 3:23: *For all have sinned and fall short of the glory of God.*

Explain the verse. State that everyone that ever lived has sinned. Ask the person: "Describe your definition of sin."

When the person is finished, ask your friend to describe whether he or she ever has sinned. If the individual says, "Yes," then move on to the next step. If "No" is the answer, then list some sins that everyone who ever has lived most certainly has committed. For example, ask whether your friend has told a lie. gotten frustrated while driving the car, or looked at someone else with lust in his or her heart (that example will take care of every man that has ever lived!) Say that *sin* simply is disobeying God.

Typically at this point the person will acknowledge his or her sin. If the person can't acknowledge this, he or she is NOT ready to get saved anyway. You cannot be saved until you know that you are lost. Now explain the CONSEQUENCES of sin.

Step 3—The Consequence

Do not hurry here. If someone does not understand that sin is a serious, personal offense against God, then that person will not see the need to be saved. This is the key reason why literally hundreds of millions of people who are Christians practice in "name only" but have no real relationship with God. They are not saved as the New Testament defines salvation. They do not understand how much of an offense they have given to a holy God. Unfortunately, for many people, Jesus subtly has been reduced to a good teacher that helps them live a moral life but is not a life-changing God that becomes the Master of everything they do.

Again, remember when this book uses the term *you* in reference to sin, remember that the proper pronoun is *we*. Always remember when witnessing that the word *we* carries more weight than does *you* or *they*.

Take your friend to Romans 6:23. Read *For the wages of sin is death but the gift of God is eternal life in Christ Jesus our Lord*.

Explain the verse by showing that we all have earned death. Highlight two words: *wages* and *death*.

For *wages* use an illustration concerning salaries. Ask whether your friend ever has worked. Ask how often payday occurred. Then ask the friend why he or she got paid. The person typically will say, "Because I earned that money." You then will reply, "The issue is the same with our sin. Because we have sinned, we have earned death.

Then explain that the word *death* refers to separation. Tell your friend that we all have a physical death in which we are separated from this life. However, death also can mean that someone can be separated from God eternally. That is a far, far worse death.

Explain that we all have a problem. The truly loving, perfect, personal God has created us to know Him. However, He also is a holy God. On earth we talk about holiness, but God is the only being that IS holy in the universe. Because of His holiness, He demands that we be in right standing with Him before we can be in His presence. We don't like to be around things that are dirty or foul. For example, do you want to be around things that evidently are physically unclean? Imagine how God feels being around sin. Sin is infinitely unclean to Him.

As a transition then say the following: "So how can we stand before a Holy God and get to spend eternity with Him in heaven?"

Step 4—The Solution

Tell your friend that God loves him or her and desires to spend eternity with that person. Consequently, God provided a way for your friend to be with Him. God had to show the ultimate sacrifice to the world so we could understand how holy He is as well as how consequential the damages are of sin.

Then read Romans 5:8: *But God demonstrates His own love toward us in that while we were still sinners, Christ died for us.*

Explain that God sent His Son to earth to show us how to live our lives on a day-to-day basis, but that was not His ultimate purpose. He died because God wanted a payment for sins. Remember, the penalty for sin is death. God sent His Son to take that payment for sins. On the cross, for the only time in eternity, God the Father and God the Son were separated spiritually as the sins of all people were placed on Christ. God knew that someone had to die for sin; in a sense, He chose Himself. Only a perfect sacrifice, freely given, was sufficient.

In transition, now ask this: "So what does that mean for you and me?"

Step 5—The Choice

Read Romans 10:9: *That if you confess with your mouth the Lord Jesus, and believe in your heart that God raised Him from the dead, you will be saved.*

Tell your friend that on the cross Christ did everything for that individual. However, Scripture repeatedly describes one action your friend must take—SURRENDERING one's life to Jesus. How does your friend do that? The person must do two things.

First: believe. Ask your friend whether he or she believes in Jesus not only as a teacher but as the Lord of the Universe.

If the answer is "no," then address that issue. Open your Bible to John 10:27-30 to show that Jesus says He is equal to the Father.

If the answer is "yes", then proceed. Say, "The second decision we must make is whether we want to call on Him as Lord."

Explain to your friend that when someone is your Lord, it means that you have totally surrendered every aspect of your life to that person. This decision typically elicits a life change. You decide to have a complete release of your time, dreams, aspirations, hopes, finances, family . . . everything.

Explain that you are not saying that God is calling everyone to surrender to Him, pack their bags, and move to the other side of the world for Him. He is, however, asking for a heart commitment.

At this point I like to share my testimony. I give my friend a brief, brief, brief summary of how 22 years ago I surrendered my life to Christ. Nothing has been the same since. Ask your friend, "Have you ever truly surrendered your life to Christ? Have you ever had a change in everything you do and think because of this?"

If people at this point say "yes," ask them to explain when and how they got saved. Try to get them to pinpoint a time for those decisions. This will cause them to reflect on whether they actually TRULY gave their lives to Christ without your having to address the issue directly. If they say "no", take them to step 6.

Step 6—The Universal Offer

Finish simply by reading Romans 10:13: *For whoever calls on the name of the Lord shall be saved.*

Tell your friend how moral or immoral he or she has been doesn't matter; if a person calls on the Lord, the Bible promises whoever does this will be saved. This is an act of humility before a perfect God. Everyone has to arrive at the point of having a contrite heart and giving his or her life to Him. Ask the friend whether he or she would consider giving his or her life to Christ.

If the answer is, "No, I'm not ready," explain that no one should feel pressured into this decision. It's a personal choice. However, again explain how much joy surrendering to Christ brought you personally. Explain to your friend that maybe God has a purpose in this conversation and that at any time you can discuss these matters further. Explain that you don't think you are better than anyone else but that this was something you had to struggle with over time. Encourage the person to talk with you further.

If the person says, "Yes, I'd like to give my life to Christ," say the following things.

a) Your friend can give his or her life to Christ right now by praying to Him.

b) You can pray with your friend, or the person can pray individually.

c) If you pray with your friend, tell him or her that you are not an intercessor; you are just helping the friend think of the words to say, because voicing this prayer may be a new concept.

d) Take the person through a prayer by having him or her repeat after you. (The prayer has no correct form or style.) Pray something such as this:

Father, I know I'm a sinner, but I know you love me. I want to surrender my life to you. Forgive me of my sins. Thank you for my salvation. In Jesus' name, Amen.

That's it, my friends. Sharing your faith doesn't take long. You have to take your friend through only a few verses. Maybe God will use you to lead your friend to Christ. At a minimum He can use you to plant a seed of truth in his or her heart. God bless YOU for your faithfulness.

Questions/Statements a Catholic Might Ask/Make
1) Are you saying that because I'm Catholic, I'm not right with God?

Your response: Not at all. You can be a Protestant, Catholic, Pentecostal, etc, and still not know the Lord. I just want to make sure all of my friends know Christ. I know that some people just go through the motions, spiritually speaking. Other people never really have thought through the consequences of their belief system. Some people just never have been shown in Scripture how to be truly saved. I'm so thankful that someone showed me. I wanted to show you as well. I hope, in turn, you pass this on to others.

2) In my heart, I feel like you must be a good person to be saved. Is that not right?

Your response: When Christ died on the cross, a criminal was being crucified next to Him. That thief called on Jesus as Lord. However, was the thief on the cross a good person? What good work had he done? He was a thief about to be crucified for a life of crime (Luke 23:39-43). If salvation depended on good works, then how do we explain the thief's salvation?

Instead, all Christ demands is a heart commitment to call Him as Lord. The thief recognized that Jesus was going to His Kingdom. He wanted to be a part of whatever Christ was doing. Salvation is by grace, not by works. However, once you give your life, God promises He will send His Spirit into your life. You will WANT to do more good works than before. Good works originate from God and not from ourselves. Do not worry. God will give you more of a heart for the poor, downtrodden, and lonely than you've ever had.

3) I feel like salvation has to be through my church.

Your response: God takes His church very seriously (Mt. 16). However, He never, ever says the church will save us. The purpose of the church is to point people to salvation (Acts 2:38-42), not to bestow salvation.

4) I feel better when I confess my sins to a priest.

Your response: You certainly can talk to people for wise counsel. However, no priest, saint, or other person can be your intercessor for your sins (1 Tim. 2:5). Only Christ is our intercessor.

5) Doesn't Mary have a role in salvation?

Your response: Mary is the most blessed of all women who have ever lived. However, even Mary knew she needed a savior. The Bible says: And Mary said: "*My soul glorifies the Lord and my spirit rejoices in God my Savior*" (Luke 1:49-50).

Mary is not God. She is not one person of the Trinity. She is a great woman who is with Her Father in heaven right now. She does not have the power or authority to help us. That power and authority is limited to God alone.

6) If I believe salvation is only through grace, can't I do whatever I want?

Your response: No, once you have given your life to Christ, the Holy Spirit will enter your life and will guide you to do things God wants you to do (Eph. 2:10). You naturally will want to do the things of God. You still will sin, because to err is human, but you will want to grow closer to Him by doing the things He likes.

7) The Catholic Church has the tradition to back up what it teaches. Your church only has been around since the 1600s. Do you mean to tell me that for 1600 years our church was wrong and yours was correct?

Your response: We don't trace our church to Martin Luther. We trace our church back to the time of Christ. Millions of wonderful believers have been part of the global church that believed in salvation through Christ alone. We hold that the Catholic Church began to lose focus for a few hundred years after the time of the Crusades. Martin Luther and other reformers chose to highlight these problems and to return to the beliefs from which the church was founded. In no way was Luther or any of the Reformers trying to say new revelation or new theology existed. They simply were trying to return to the very truths that your forefathers held dear.

8) Are you saying that tradition plays no part in what we should believe?

Your response: We're not saying that at all. We only are saying that Scripture was divinely inspired by God (2 Tim. 3:16). The early church fathers—Jerome, Augustine, Athanasius, Origen, Ignatius—all believed in the authority of Scripture. They didn't deny that God used the church. However, they believed that Scripture was the ultimate authority. So do we. If tradition contrasts with Scripture, we should side with Scripture.

May God bless you as you minister to your Catholic friends. I pray you will share with them in a manner that is humble and gracious. My prayer is that the Holy Spirit will guide you in all you do.

[1]Crone, Patricia, *Cambridge Illustrated History: Islamic World*, Francis Robinson, ed., Cambridge: Cambridge University Press. 1996, 2.

[2]Official Catholic doctrine has not yet elevated Mary to divine status. However in practice, millions of Catholics around the world basically venerate Mary on the same level of Christ.

[3]*http://www.americancatholic.org/features/special/default.aspx?id=29*

[4]Blackaby, Henry, *Experiencing God*, Nashville: B&H Publishing, 2008, 84.

Chapter 4

How to Witness
to Your Protestant Friends

How would a person go about defining a *Protestant*? This actually is a more difficult question than you might think. Protestants typically are thought of as believers that split off from the Catholic Church starting from the year 1517 when Martin Luther nailed the 95 theses on the church door in Wittenberg. He wasn't trying to start a new church but just wanted to reform the church he loved. He wasn't the first reformer and certainly wasn't the only one, either. Men like Luther, John Calvin, and John Knox helped give birth to Presbyterian, Lutheran, and all manner of Reformed churches. From Ulrich Zwingli indirectly sprang churches such as the Amish, the Hutterites, and the Mennonites. As the reformation spread to England, we begin to see Anglican and then eventually Baptist and Methodist churches forming. Finally from the Baptists we can see the Churches of Christ; from the Methodists we can see a grand variety of the Holiness/Pentecostal churches. Of course, the churches listed represent only a fraction of the total Protestant churches in the world.

All of these churches would state that they did not form in the 1600s-1900s; instead, they merely were reactions to poor theology that formed in the Catholic Church. None of these churches were birthed from "new" revelations as the Jehovah's Witnesses or Mormons were. They simply represent an attempt to remedy divergent theology or worship styles that had been built into the Catholic Church. Protestants consider each other "brothers and sisters" and have only minor differences in theology and liturgy.[1]

However, no matter what denomination an individual claims, for the purposes of this chapter, if your friend doesn't know Christ as Lord and Savior and hasn't experienced a changed life that bears evident fruit for Jesus, that person is a "nominal" (in-name-only) Protestant.

With all these denominations, you would think that the task of spreading the gospel is complete and that this chapter is unnecessary. After all, estimates tell us that 32.29 percent of the world is Christian.[2] I'd like you to think about that statistic logically. Do we really think that one-third of the world has proclaimed Jesus Christ as Lord and Savior? Countries such as the United States, Brazil, South Korea, South Africa, Kenya, and Nigeria all have high numbers of Christians; yet in each of these societies sexual promiscuity is evident, crime is rampant, and churches (overall) appear incredibly weak. In other words, you can have the title *Christian*, *Catholic*, or *Evangelical* in front of your name, but that does not mean you know Christ. Don't be lulled into believing that since a plethora of denominations exist, the world is reached. The world is far from reached for Christ. Unfortunately one area we have to target is right here in the middle of the "Christian" world.

As a pastor, the most common question I receive is, "How do I know that I'm saved?" When that question is posed, I take the inquirer to Scripture. I then show him or her that people can know they are saved by not only a past declaration for Christ but also by their present fruitfulness for Him.[3] However, ultimately, I can't dogmatically with 100-percent certainly tell someone whether that person is saved. The truth is, even we ourselves don't really know our hearts (Jer. 17:9). If we don't really know ourselves, then how can we possibly judge others when salvation is concerned? God, in His grace, is the judge; I am not.

This realization that I am not the judge of others is one of the most freeing moments in evangelism. When I witness, I don't feel as though I am the judge or the jury; I'm just the messenger. I tell the story. I solve this problem of "who is saved and who is not" by just making sure I tell everyone the message. I'm not picky. If you are my friend, I'm going to make sure that I've talked to you about Christ—regardless of your denominational affiliation.

When you visit with someone who is a nominal Protestant, I advise you to witness to that person in much the same way I described in the chapter on Catholicism. In many ways you have the same advantages with a nominal Protestant as you would with a Catholic. As a basis Protestants have a belief in God, Jesus, the Holy Spirit, sin, and the Bible. These beliefs quickly enable you to establish more common ground.

In the end, however, when you witness to a nominal Protestant, spend more time on the aspect of LIFE CHANGE. Let's reflect on this truth. If no life change has occurred, is your friend saved, or is your friend like Nicodemus? In the Scriptures Nicodemus is a moral, good man who knows the law (John 3:1-21). Nicodemus, however, is so unsure of the Lordship of Christ, for fear of being seen he can approach Him only at night. Nicodemus is close to the kingdom of God, but he is not there yet.

How Do I Witness to My Protestant Friends?

(If you are reading the entire book, you quickly may skim the first four steps, as they are the same in many of the chapters. Also, step five in this plan is very similar to the chapter on Catholicism. However, be aware of some key differences in the process as well.)

Step 1—Befriend them.

Do not befriend people for the purpose of witnessing to them.

Befriend a colleague because the person is created by God and is of infinite importance. That alone makes him or her worthy of your time and/or money investment in his or her life.

How do you befriend them? People want to know that they are of value. Time investment is far more important than is financial investment. Find ways initially to spend time with your friends. Take them out to eat or invite them for a meal in your home. Drink coffee with them. Offer to help the person with an errand or household need. Watch a baseball game with the person. Make the person aware that you care by putting a time investment in him or her.

Step 2—Avoid the urge to just be their friend and never engage in a spiritual conversation.

Don't be afraid to put yourself out there. Make sure, after you determine that you are going to share your faith, that you slip into conversation something about God, church, or Jesus. Let this friend know that you are a spiritual person. You subtly are letting this individual know that God is important to you.

Step 3—Look for the spiritual clues.

Only God can do certain things. For example, only God can convict us of sin (John 16:8) and draw people to Himself (John 12:32). People don't just seek God on their own (Rom. 3). When someone mentions God or sin, then I know that, at a minimum, God is working on the person's heart. After all, only God can cause us to become convicted of sin or to think about Him. This is an open door to step into what God already is accomplishing. If I hear a friend talking on any of these topics, you better believe that very quickly thereafter I'll be saying, "May I share something with you (about Christ). . .?"

Step 4—Seize the initiative, even if spiritual clues do not present themselves.

Let's be honest: much of the time people do not make their spiritual needs plainly evident. In that case use a list of spiritual questions to inject spirituality in the conversation. In *Experiencing God* Henry Blackaby gave a list of excellent lead-in questions. Questions in conversation could include:

- Do you want to talk about what is happening in your life?
- What do you see as the greatest challenge in your life?
- What is the most significant thing happening in your life now?
- How can I pray for you?
- Would you tell me what God is doing in your life?
- What is God bringing to the surface in your life?
- What particular burden has God given you?[4]

If none of these questions fits your personality type, you can try something a bit more innocuous.

For example, if over coffee you are meeting with your friend and the Spirit has shown you that the time is right to share with your friend, you can say,

"(Friend), may I ask you a personal question?"

If the friend says "Yes", then say,

"You and I have known each other for a while. Something is kind of important to me. Do you believe in something after this life?"

With a Protestant, you might want to add, "Do you know for certain that if you died today, you will go to heaven?"

These questions do not limit you to one denomination or even one religion. They are fair questions that in our culture are not too intrusive. Be prepared to let the friend talk. In fact, the friend might talk for a while. With Protestants you may hear some very divergent answers. Whatever they say, treat them with respect, because THEY DESERVE RESPECT.

Whether the person says "Yes" or "No" to the question, bridge the conversation with this statement:

"(Friend), I believe in something after this life. I really have confidence in what will happen to me after I die. May I share with you something that has truly impacted me?"

If you feel him or her get defensive or sense that the person doesn't want to hear the answer, explain that you don't want to push but that something really did change your life. You are open to sharing that fact at any time.

If your friend appears to be ready to hear your answer, say something along these lines:

"_____ years ago I gave my life to Christ. I cannot tell you how much this decision has changed everything about me. In fact, nothing about me is the same since that decision. Have you ever made a decision for God that changed everything about your life?" (ALTERNATE QUESTION: "If you were to die today, do you know for CERTAIN that you'd spend eternity in heaven?") Take a moment to let the person respond. Then you have arrived at the core question of the entire process. Ask your friend:

"May I show you from Scripture how you may make a life-changing decision for Christ as well?" (Alternate response: "The Bible shows us how we can be certain that we'll spend eternity in heaven? May I show you what it says?")

If your friend says "yes", follow the next steps.

If the person says "no", thank him or her for listening, explain as a friend that you are ready to talk on this topic at any time; then move on.

The key centers on GIVING YOUR FRIEND OPPORTUNITIES TO BE IN CONTROL. People in this generation of Americans, Brazilians, Africans, etc., do not particularly want you to force them to do anything. However, if they give permission to share, then they will have far more open ears to hear.

5) Sharing the plan of salvation in six easy steps
Step 1—The Source

Take out your pocket New Testament. Tell your friend you want to show six verses from Scripture (Be sure you are developing the habit of carrying a pocket New Testament.) Explain that you don't want to preach, but you just want to show from the Bible why you have joy now and why, if you died today, you know you will go to heaven. Open your Bible to the book of 1 John 5:13 and read:

I write these things to you who believe in the name of the Son of God so that you may know that you have eternal life (1 John 5:13, NIV).

Explain that God actually wrote the Bible so that billions of individuals can know how they can have eternal life. The Bible is a love letter to your friend because God wants him or her to know Him. Scripture says He already knows us, but He wants us to know Him.

Step 2—The Problem

Turn in the Bible to Romans 3:23: *For all have sinned and fall short of the glory of God.*

Explain the verse. State that everyone that ever lived has sinned. Ask the person: "Describe your definition of *sin.*"

When the person is finished, ask your friend to describe whether he or she ever has sinned. If the individual says, "Yes," then move on to the next step. If "No" is the answer, then list some sins that everyone who ever has lived most certainly has committed. For example, ask whether your friend has told a lie. gotten frustrated while driving the car, or looked at someone else with lust in his or her heart. Say that sin is simply disobeying God.

Typically at this point the person will acknowledge his or her sin. If the person can't acknowledge this, he or she is NOT ready to get saved anyway. You cannot be saved until you know that you are lost. Now explain the CONSEQUENCES of sin.

Step 3—The Consequence

Do not hurry here. If someone does not understand that sin is a serious, personal offense against God, then that person will not see the need to be saved. This is the key reason why literally hundreds of millions of people are Christians in "name only". They do not understand how much of an offense they have given to a holy God. They see Jesus as a good teacher that helps them live moral lives but not a life-changing God that becomes the Master of everything they do.

Again, remember when this book uses the term "you" in reference to sin, remember that the proper pronoun is "we". Always remember when witnessing that the word "we" carries more weight than does "you" or "they".

Take your friend to Romans 6:23: *For the wages of sin is death but the gift of God is eternal life in Christ Jesus our Lord.*

Explain the verse by showing that we have all earned death. Highlight two words: *wages* and *death*.

For *wages* use an illustration about salaries. Ask whether your friend ever has worked. Ask how often payday occurred. Then ask the friend why he or she got paid. The person typically will say, "Because I earned that money." You then will reply, "The issue is the same with our sin. Because we have sinned, we have earned death.

Then explain that the word *death* refers to separation. Tell your friend that we all have a physical death in which we are separated from this life. However, death also can mean that someone can be separated from God eternally. That is a far, far worse death.

Explain that we all have a problem. The truly loving, perfect, personal God has created us to know Him. However, He also is a holy God. On earth we talk about holiness, but in the universe God is the only being that IS holy. Because of His holiness He demands that we be in right standing with Him before we can be in His presence. We don't like to be around things that are dirty or foul. For example, do you want to be around someone who is really foul-mouthed? Do you want to be around things that evidently are physically unclean? Imagine how a perfect, holy God feels being around sin. To God sin is unclean.

As a transition then say the following: "So how can we stand before a holy God and get to spend eternity with Him in heaven?"

Step 4—The Solution

Tell your friend that God loves him or her and desires to spend eternity with that person. Consequently, God provides a way for your friend to be with Him. He provides a way to sacrifice Himself for our salvation.

Then read Romans 5:8: *But God demonstrates His own love toward us in that while we were still sinners, Christ died for us.* Explain that God sends His Son to earth to show us how to live our lives on a day-to-day basis, but that is not His ultimate purpose. He died because God wants a payment for sins. Remember, the penalty for sin is death. God sends His Son to take that payment for sins.

On the cross, for the only time in eternity, God the Father and God the Son are separated spiritually as the sins of all people are placed on Christ. God knows that someone has to die for sin; in a sense, He chooses Himself. Only a perfect sacrifice, freely given, is sufficient.

That sacrifice is not an action, another person, or a church's activities, but it is Christ. Put simply, the point of Jesus' being sent to earth is that He died on the cross, was buried for three days, and then rose again to live in YOUR life.

In transition, now ask this: "So what does that mean for you and me?"

Step 5 — The Choice

In Romans 10:9 the Bible says: *That if you confess with your mouth the Lord Jesus, and believe in your heart that God has raised Him from the dead, you will be saved.*

Tell your friend that on the cross Christ does everything for us. However, Scripture repeatedly describes one action your friend must take — SURRENDER his or her life to Jesus. How does your friend do that? The person must do two things.

First: believe. Ask your friend whether he or she believes in Jesus not only as a teacher but as the Lord of the Universe.

If the answer is "no," then address that issue. Open your Bible to John 10:27-30 and show that Jesus says He is equal to the Father.

If the answer is "yes", then proceed. Say, "The second decision which we must make is whether we want to call Him as Lord."

Explain to your friend that when someone is your Lord, this means that you have totally surrendered every aspect of your life to that person. This decision typically elicits a life change. After all, if you are willing to say your dreams, hopes, money, time, etc., are going to be someone else's, that is going to bring about a change.

Explain that you are not saying that God is calling everyone to surrender to Him, pack their bags, and move overseas for Him. He is, however, asking for a heart commitment.

At this point I like to share my testimony. I give my friend a brief, brief, brief summary of how 22 years ago I surrendered my life to Christ and state that nothing has been the same since.

AT THIS POINT, WE DIVERGE FROM THE PATH WE READ IN THE LAST CHAPTER. I ENCOURAGE YOU TO TAKE YOUR FRIEND THROUGH THE BOOK OF 1 JOHN AND LOOK AT HOW WE CAN KNOW WHETHER WE HAVE CHRIST IN US. ASK YOU FRIEND WHETHER YOU CAN READ JUST A FEW MORE VERSES. YOU MAY OR MAY NOT WANT TO USE ALL OF THESE. SEVERAL PROBABLY WILL BE SUFFICIENT.

1) *If we claim to have fellowship with him and yet walk in the darkness, we lie and do not live out the truth* (1 John 1:6, NIV).

2) *We know that we have come to know him if we keep his commands* (1 John 2:3).

3) *Anyone who claims to be in the light but hates a brother or sister is still in the darkness* (1 John 2:9, NIV).

4) *If anyone loves the world, the love of the Father is not in him. For all that* is *in the world—the lust of the flesh, the lust of the eyes, and the pride of life—is not of the Father but is of the world* (1 John 2:15-16).

5) *Whoever denies the Son does not have the Father either* (1 John 2:23, NIV, referring to the Son's deity)

6) *No one who is born of God will continue to sin, because God's seed remains in them; they cannot go on sinning, because they have been born of God.* (1 John 3:9, NIV — Sinning here implies repetitive, unrepentant sinning.)

7) *If anyone has material possessions and sees a brother or sister in need but has no pity on him, how can the love of God be in that him? Dear children, let us not love with words or tongue but with actions and in truth* (1 John 3:17).

Tell your friend that you are not picking these verses out of a hat. You only are asking the person the same type of questions you asked yourself. Ask whether these verses describe his or her life with Christ?

Tell your friend that you know that he or she is moral (if that is the case). Tell your friend that you respect him or her. You only are asking the person to examine his or her beliefs as to whether the person really has made the most important decision in life.

Ask your friend, "Have you ever truly surrendered your life to Christ? Have you experienced a change in everything you do, plan, and think because of this decision for Him?"

If the friend says "yes," ask the person to explain how and when this occurred. Try to get a life-changing experience with Christ pinpointed.

If the individual says "no," go to step 6.

Step 6—The Universal Offer

Finish simply by reading Romans 10:13: *For whoever calls on the name of the Lord shall be saved.*

Tell your friend how moral or immoral someone has been doesn't matter; if a person calls on the Lord, the Bible promises whoever does this will be saved. This is an act of humility before a perfect God. Everyone has to arrive at the point of having a contrite heart and giving his or her life to Him. Ask the friend whether the person would consider giving his or her life to Christ.

If the answer is, "No, I'm not ready," explain that no one should feel pressured into this decision. It's a personal choice. However, again explain how much joy surrendering to Christ has brought you personally. Explain to your friend that maybe God has a purpose in this conversation and that you can discuss these matters further at any time. Explain that you don't think you are better than anyone else but that this was something you had to struggle with over time. Encourage the person to talk with you further.

Advise your friend to read 1 John for himself or herself. Tell the person that 1 John contains only five chapters. Reading the whole book shouldn't take more than a couple of days at 10 minutes a day of reading.

If the person says, "Yes, I'd like to give my life to Christ," say the following things.

a) Your friend can give his or her life to Christ right now by praying to Him.

b) You can pray with your friend, or the person can pray individually.

c) If you pray with your friend, tell him or her that you are not an intercessor; you are just helping the friend think of the words to say, because voicing this prayer may be a new concept.

d) Take the person through a prayer by having him or her repeat after you. (The prayer doesn't have to be in any specific form or style.) Pray something such as this:

Father, I know I'm a sinner, but I know you love me. I want to surrender my life to you. Forgive me of my sins. Thank you for my salvation. In Jesus' name, Amen.

Questions/Statements a Nominal Protestant Might Ask/Make
1) Are you saying that I'm a worse sinner than you?

Your response: No, not at all. We all are sinners. In fact, the safest way to remember how badly we are as sinners is to remember how Paul describes himself: *This is a faithful saying and worthy of all acceptance, that Christ Jesus came into the world to save sinners, of whom I am chief* (1 Tim. 1:15).

2) All my life I have been a good Baptist, Methodist, Assembly of God member, or Episcopalian. Why do you think I need to do this?

Your response: First of all, no one truly is "good" (Mt. 19:17). Secondly, what I think doesn't matter. I had to sit down and think through this issue for myself. I'm only asking you to do the same.

I wouldn't share this with you if I didn't care about you and want the same fulfillment I have.

3) A lot of people have acted worse than me. Why should I have to do this?

Your response: Scripture is full of people who acted badly but who realized they needed to REPENT. Repentance means turning from one's sins to God. Noah, Moses, Abraham, David, and Peter all start out badly but turn to give their lives to God. However, even moral people have to repent as well. Paul says no one has been more righteous than he. Yet he still has to turn and give his life to God.

See what Paul says: *If anyone else thinks he may have confidence in the flesh, I more so: circumcised the eighth day, of the stock of Israel, of the tribe of Benjamin, a Hebrew of the Hebrews; concerning the law, a Pharisee; concerning zeal, persecuting the church; concerning the righteousness which is in the law, blameless. But what things were gain to me, these I have counted loss for Christ* (Phil. 3:4b-7).

4) We live in a world that is a more scientific age. I believe that Jesus is just a man but that His moral teachings are good.

Your response: In Scripture we see that Jesus Himself claims He is God. The Bible is clear that we cannot view Christ as just a human being.

Who is a liar but he who denies that Jesus is the Christ? He is antichrist who denies the Father and the Son. Whoever denies the Son does not have the Father either; he who acknowledges the Son has the Father also (1 John 2:22-23).

If Jesus is God, then we must do what He says: "*But why do you call me 'Lord, Lord' and not do the things which I say?*" (Luke 6:46).

What does Jesus want us to do? Recognize His Lordship in our lives.

When Jesus came into the region of Caesarea Philippi, He asked His disciples, saying, "Who do men say that I, the Son of Man, am? So they said, "Some say John the Baptist, some Elijah, and others Jeremiah or one of the prophets." He said to them, "But who do you say that I am?" Simon Peter answered and said, "You are the Christ, the Son of the living God." Jesus answered and said to him, "Blessed are you, Simon Bar-Jonah, for flesh and blood has not revealed this to you, but My Father who is in heaven" (Mt. 16:13-17).

5) Give me some time to think about this decision. I'll do it some day.

Your response: You might need to take some time. However, do not plan for good things for tomorrow and neglect what God wants you to do today. The Bible says: *Come now, you who say, "Today or tomorrow we will go to such and such a city, spend a year there, buy and sell, and make a profit"; whereas you do not know what will happen tomorrow. For what is your life? It is even a vapor that appears for a little time and then vanishes away. Instead you ought to say, "If the Lord wills, we shall live and do this or that." But now you boast in your arrogance. All such boasting is evil* (Jas. 4:13-16).

6) I believe that if we are sincere, we'll make it to heaven, no matter what religion we are.

Your response: The truth is, no religion will get us to heaven. Only an exclusive RELATIONSHIP with Jesus Christ will enable us to get to heaven (Rom. 10:9).

May God bless you in your endeavor to witness to your friends. Remember the following words from Scripture: *For God has not given us a spirit of fear, but of power and of love and of a sound mind* (2 Tim. 1:7). Let HIM work through you.

[1]For a phenomenal overview of denominations in the U.S. see *Handbook of Denominations in the United States*—13th edition by Frank Mead.

[2]Mandryk, Jason, *Operation World: The Definitive Prayer Guide to Every Nation*, Intervarsity Press, Downers Grove, IL, 2010, 2. These statistics include all churches affiliated with Christianity—Catholic, Orthodox, Protestant, Evangelical, Pentecostal—as well as a variety of other churches that are on the fringe of typical Christian beliefs.

[3]If someone asks you that question, use the book of 1 John. A quick read will show you that John's purpose is to give readers an overview of how they can know they are saved.

[4]Blackaby, *Experiencing God*, 84.

Chapter 5

How to Witness to Your Animistic Friends

What is the largest religion in the world? Is it Christianity? No. Is it Islam? No.

The largest religion in the world is *animism*. Animism occurs in a variety of forms. In Haiti one might call it *voodoo*. In Brazil one might call it *Candomble*, *Umbanda,* or *Macumba*. In Africa the religion might manifest in a variety of ways. People might use a witch doctor, amulets, evil eye, or a variety of other means to try to manipulate the spirits for their own power. In India some might be a Hindu in name, but in actual practice they are more animistic.

You might ask, "Why include this religion in this book?" First, I've become convinced that if animism is as predominant as statistics show, the typical believer needs to know something about this religion. Secondly, since in our midst we have people from all over the world, the time is right to start reaching them in their heart languages and from their heart religions. In our cities we have many friends from Asia, Africa, South (and North) America who have animistic influences in their lives. The time has arrived for us to know how to target this significant segment of the world's population.

Background

Animism is a broad term dealing with the interaction of the spirit world. The practice has no scriptural text to follow, nor do we know any principal founder of animistic belief. In like manner animism has no founding date or history to trace the belief system with any certainty.

However, for millennia people from all over the world have followed animistic practices. Followers of other religions also can be practitioners of animism with no inconsistency. This is the concept of being a "folk" practitioner. For example, an estimated 70 percent of Muslims are "folk" Muslims.[1] Folk Muslims believe in the core tenets of Orthodox Islam, but in daily practice they observe animistic practices. For example, these Muslims believe evil spirits or "jinn" affect the way they live their daily lives. They work to manipulate these "jinn".

Christians often unwittingly utilize animistic practices. Do you doubt that many Christians have allowed animistic practices to fall into their daily routine? Have you ever knocked on wood for good luck? For a moment think about that action. Why would knocking on wood affect your luck? Is the wood affecting your daily activities? Do you have a lucky shirt you use before a sporting event? What do you think is the origin of that luck? Do you really believe that thinking the shirt will affect the outcome of a game is biblical? On a subconscious level you are trying to have inanimate objects affect the world around you. Those are forms of animism. On a more obvious level, if people use a Ouija board or a séance, then they certainly are dealing with animism.

These are minor examples of animistic thought. After all, where does Scripture state that items or actions can manipulate your fortune? Ultimately, God is in control of our daily lives. If we walk under a ladder or break a mirror, this really does not affect what is going to happen one minute later in our lives (except that you will have to clean up the broken pieces).

So what does having interaction with the spirit world mean? In America many people are uncomfortable with certain aspects of the spirit world. If we want to discuss God, especially in a generic sense, most Westerners will admit to some belief in a supernatural Being. If the discussion moves to an absolute evil being, 75 percent of Americans believe in the probability of the devil.[2] Beyond God and the devil, Westerners don't talk much about the spirit world. We mention angels or demons only if we are playing a video game or watching a movie. The thought that other entities in the universe might have roles in our lives doesn't cross our minds too often.

In much of the world people are very comfortable talking about far more than just God or the devil. They are very comfortable talking about the "middle level of reality" of angels, demons, and spirits. They openly believe that this middle level (the first level being an all-powerful deity, the third level being humanity, and the middle level being the spirit world) can be manipulated for their own benefit.[3]

As a reminder, an animist believes that you can utilize the spirit world either for good or bad. Consequently, through rituals and core beliefs, animists attempt to interact with the spirit world for their own purposes. This belief system manifests differently in different areas of the world.

How Does One Interact with the Spirit World?

You can understand how an animist interacts with the spirit world by remembering a few key terms. Because this belief system has no Scripture, no organizational structure, and no founder, we will have to describe animism in general themes.

The first of these themes is *manipulation*. Animists will try to utilize a spirit for their own betterment. For example, one might offer sacrifices to a specific supernatural being to get a better job, be cured of diseases, or receive any myriad of blessings. In America we see the term *witch doctor* and think this is only a theatrical term from the movies. In truth, hundreds of millions of people around the world believe a witch doctor can manipulate the spirit world for their own benefit. Closer to home, as the Western shift to New Age ideology continues, terms such as *channeling the spirit world* bear a striking resemblance to this idea.

To their dismay many missionaries in Africa have observed individuals, in whom they have invested many years of their lives for the church, naturally going back to the witch doctor when they have a sickness. Often this is because the Christianity the Africans have been taught left no room for the spirit world to interact with their daily lives. They are taught that God is the Creator and Redeemer, but is He really the Healer as well? Scripture says God heals, but many Africans are taught the Western, secular mindset that only medicine heals. In truth, healing occurs from a mixture of both the sacred and secular.

The second term is *power*. This term is similar to manipulation. Animists seek to utilize the spirit world for their own power. Practitioners of Candomble and Macumba in South America tap into the spirit world and experience well-documented possessions. Adherents seek out the experience of possession because doing so makes them feel powerful. An adherent can have power over another person as well. In fact, the very basis of hexes and voodoo centers on gaining power over another person.

The third term is *fear*. We will use this term as a bridge to the gospel. People seek out the spirit world either because they are afraid of the day-to-day problems of life, or they seek out the spirit world because they fear not pacifying the spirits in their lives. In the end, as practitioners try to control their spirits for their own betterment, they become controlled by fear themselves.

Acknowledgement that fear is the core of the belief system of animists has caused missionaries around the world to have great success in reaching these people. We can do the same thing not only with strict animists but with Muslims, Christians, or practitioners of any other religion that spend their day-to-day lives practicing animism under the guise of being involved in their own religion.

The fourth term is *pragmatism*.[4] Animism is a belief system that "works". It is not based on logic or any sacred texts; it is based on the fact that it appears to function in a person's daily life. One would be hard-pressed to find an animist who would systematically defend his or her belief system. Most practices and beliefs are adopted from the environment and even handed down informally for generations. For this reason Christian apologetics (arguments to defend the faith) usually do not work well with the animist. The Christian witness must show how the Lord God is a personal Being and reigns over the cosmos and everything in it. It must not focus on a point-by-point apologetic of Christian theology.

Animists who actually are adherents of other religions such as Islam or Hinduism often demonstrate their spiritual affinity through their words, actions, and even jewelry. Even though they might externally state they believe in fundamentals of another faith, they actually believe true power springs from what they wear or say. This "power" can originate from a cross around the neck to a charm hanging from the window of the car to the mentioning of God when communicating future plans. Many Evangelicals, especially from the West, look at these manifestations and think that animists truly are committed to "high religion" such as Catholicism or Islam. The reality, however, is that they utilize these items and rituals for their personal benefit; they usually do this without much reflection. They do so because it works for them.

How to Witness to an Animist

Let's examine some ways to begin the conversation with an animist. As with all other overviews in this book, you can read pages 33-37 to get a more detailed overview of steps 1 through 4. However, what approaches can we take to lead our friends to Christ?

1) Befriend them.
2) Avoid the urge to **just** be their friend and never engage in a spiritual conversation.
3) Look for the spiritual clues.
4) Seize the initiative even if spiritual clues do not present themselves.

Again, you can re-examine the previous chapters "How to Share Your Faith with Your Catholic Friends" or "How to Share Your Faith with Your Protestant Friends" to get a detailed list of lead-in questions you can use to bridge the gap between yourself and an animist. However, you have other options you might use. (These additional questions all assume that the animist will have a belief in a higher power. Most animists will believe in a higher power.)

Let's imagine I'm trying to start a dialogue with a friend who is an animist. After a few minutes of typical conversation I would ask a lead-in question such as:

• Do you feel content with your relationship with God?
• Do you believe that God, your Creator, is pleased with you?
• In your view how does one walk with God and receive grace and protection from Him?
• Do you believe the Creator God has little control in helping you over some spirits?
• Do you believe that one day you will be with your Creator God in heaven, where He lives and reigns?
• May I explain to you how the Bible tells us we can walk

with God and be with Him forever here on this earth as well as in death?[5]

These questions all act as bridges to get this person to think on spiritual issues.

After you ask a few questions to move a conversation toward spiritual issues, you can take the following approaches to sharing your faith. I have interviewed three very godly men to ask what steps they take to discuss Christ. You can choose the approach that seems the most comfortable for you and your friend.

(Option 1)

David Bledsoe, a missionary in Brazil with the International Mission Board, has extensive experience researching as well as sharing his faith with practitioners of forms of animism. He has experience specifically with Candomble, Macumba, and Umbanda. When asked how he would continue the conversation with animists, he gave the following advice.[6] Bledsoe stated:

"Here are a few biblical teachings and passages that one can consider inserting and emphasizing when sharing the gospel with an animist. Remember, an animist usually is not thinking about the afterlife but his life in the present. Therefore, you may continue to emphasize the afterlife, but you must deal with the hear-and-now as well. One of the best themes in Scripture to use is the kingdom of God (the reign of God in both our hearts and in the universe). You can show the practitioner how to be released from darkness and dominion of Satan to God's kingdom through the gospel (i.e. Jesus)."

Bledsoe described four themes one can follow in witnessing and verses you can use to describe these truths. Take your Bible and show your friend the following ideas:

1. "Tell your friend that he or she can be free from the

evil forces that are feared." Conversion to Jesus brings God's Spirit (the Holy Spirit) into your life and therefore gives you absolute protection from Satan and evil forces."

Read and explain the following verses. Bledsoe has given you a list of possible verses that clearly show the animist the power of the One True God. Show your friend that once you are in Christ, no forces are powerful enough to take your friend away from the all-powerful God.

The Spirit you received does not make you slaves, so that you live in fear again; rather, the Spirit you received brought about your adoption to sonship. And by him we cry, "Abba, Father." The Spirit himself testifies with our spirit that we are God's children. Now if we are children, then we are heirs —heirs of God and co-heirs with Christ, if indeed we share in his sufferings in order that we may also share in his glory (Rom. 8:15-17, NIV)

We know that anyone born of God does not continue to sin; the One who was born of God keeps them safe, and the evil one cannot harm them (1 John 5:18, NIV).

So we say with confidence, "The Lord is my helper; I will not be afraid. What can mere mortals do to me?" (Heb. 13:6, NIV).

"My sheep listen to my voice; I know them, and they follow me. I give them eternal life, and they shall never perish; no one will snatch them out of my hand. My Father, who has given them to me, is greater than all ; no one can snatch them out of my Father's hand" (John 10:27-29, NIV).

2. "Tell your friend that when one enters the kingdom of God, Satan and other spirits can touch him or her only with God's permission."

. . . Therefore, in order to keep me from becoming conceited, I was given a thorn in my flesh, a messenger of Satan, to torment me. Three times I pleaded with the Lord to take it away from me. But he said to me, "My grace is sufficient for you, for my power is made perfect in weakness." Therefore I will boast all the more gladly about my weaknesses, so that Christ's power may rest on me. That is why, for Christ's sake, I delight in weaknesses, in insults, in hardships, in persecutions, in difficulties. For when I am weak, then I am strong (2 Cor. 12:7-10, NIV).

See Job 1 and 2 for another example. Satan did bring havoc and suffering in Job's life but only with God's permission. Therefore, even though Satan is described as a devouring lion, he is on a tight leash which God controls.

3. "When one receives Jesus as Lord and Mediator, the person now has access directly to the living God and does not need to return to living a life of fear and satisfying spirits."

Because our gospel came to you not simply with words but also with power, with the Holy Spirit and deep conviction. You know how we lived among you for your sake. You became imitators of us and of the Lord, for you welcomed the message in the midst of severe suffering with the joy given by the Holy Spirit.

And so you became a model to all the believers in Macedonia and Achaia. The Lord's message rang out from you not only in Macedonia and Achaia —your faith in God has become known everywhere. Therefore we do not need to say anything about it, for they themselves report what kind of reception you gave us. They tell how you turned to God from idols to serve the living and true God, and to wait for his Son from heaven, whom he raised from the dead—Jesus, who rescues us from the coming wrath (1 Thess. 1:5-10, NIV).

Therefore, since we have a great high priest who has ascended into heaven, Jesus the Son of God, let us hold firmly to the faith we profess.

For we do not have a high priest who is unable to empathize with our weaknesses, but we have one who has been tempted in every way, just as we are—yet he did not sin. Let us then approach God's throne of grace with confidence, so that we may receive mercy and find grace to help us in our time of need (Heb. 4:14-16, NIV).

4. "When one receives the gospel, he or she should continue to grow in faith and worship of Jesus and reject the temptation to return to old animistic practices."

So then, just as you received Christ Jesus as Lord, continue to live your lives in him, rooted and built up in him, strengthened in the faith as you were taught, and overflowing with thankfulness. See to it that no one takes you captive through hollow and deceptive philosophy, which depends on human tradition and the elemental spiritual forces of this world rather than on Christ. For in Christ all the fullness of the Deity lives in bodily form, and in Christ you have been brought to fullness. He is the head over every power and authority (Col. 2:6-10, NIV).

So I say, walk by the Spirit, and you will not gratify the desires of the flesh.

For the flesh desires what is contrary to the Spirit, and the Spirit what is contrary to the flesh. They are in conflict with each other, so that you are not to do whatever you want. But if you are led by the Spirit, you are not under the law.

The acts of the flesh are obvious: sexual immorality, impurity and debauchery; idolatry and witchcraft; hatred, discord, jealousy, fits of rage, selfish ambition, dissensions, factions and envy;

drunkenness, orgies, and the like. I warn you, as I did before, that those who live like this will not inherit the kingdom of God (Gal. 5:16-21, NIV).

If you can take the animist through these four ideas with complimentary verses, then you can be ready to explain how the person can give his or her life to Jesus. As a reminder simply read the verses Bledsoe has given, explain the verses in your own words, and move on to the next verse.

At this point, you can take the animist through the simple six-verse plan that has been given in the Protestant and Catholic chapters. If you need to see this plan in further detail to get ideas for transitional sentences and illustrations, please reference "Sharing the Plan of Salvation in Six Easy Steps" (pages 37-42; 52-58) in both the chapters on Protestantism and Catholicism.

• Romans 3:23 — Show your animist friend that you and he or she both are sinners.

• Romans 6:23 — Show your animist friend that our sins are very serious and that you both face consequences for those sins.

• Romans 5:8 — Show your animist friend that God was sent to earth and has given His life as a perfect sacrifice for your friend and you. This is the only sacrifice that will actually rid a person of sin, fear, and guilt.

• Romans 10:9 — Describe how your friend must commit all FEARS, hopes, everything . . *everything* . . . to Christ as Lord and Savior.

• Romans 10:13 — Promise your friend that no matter what we have done, the Bible assures us that if we've given our lives to Christ, we will be saved.

(Option 2)
Dr. Stan May was a professor at Mid-America Baptist Theo-

logical Seminary in Memphis. For six years he was in Zimbabwe and worked with people from an African animistic background. Dr. May shared an example of a conversation with an African; from this example someone might pattern a witness. I have included Dr. May's conversation, with some additional notes, to help the reader understand WHY he said what he said in the conversation. In parentheses I will include additional clarifying thoughts. Remember, as with Bledsoe's conversation, the assumption is that you already have laid some groundwork with the individual in terms of a relationship.

Dr. May said: "Traditional religionists (sometimes called *animists, dynamists*, or any number of other names) basically hold to a high god who created everything (who is distant and generally uninvolved), a pantheon of spirits, witches, ancestors, and curses that demand regular appeasement and thus create a climate of fear, and a system of power to address that fear. The great joy of the gospel is that it addresses not only the guilt of Western culture but also the shame of Middle Eastern and Eastern cultures and the fear of traditional cultures. The following dialogue takes place over a time period because traditional peoples are not in a hurry and generally will not respond to a brief encounter in a way that will produce deep-level change."[7]

Me: Greetings, Baba (Father, a term of respect)!

TR (Traditional Religionist): Greetings to you as well! How are you?

Me: Well; and how are you? (Dr. May takes a moment to show authentic concern for a person's life)

TR: We are well. How is your family?

Me: They also are well. May I inquire of yours?

TR: They are well. How is the weather in your area?

Me: We have been having good rains; and have you seen the rains?

TR: Yes, we too are having good rains. How are the crops?

Me: The crops in our area are doing well.

TR: That is good news. The crops in our area are doing well, also.

Me: Baba, I do appreciate the opportunity to visit with you in your home. I would like to ask permission to talk with you about the message that the God of the Bible has sent me to proclaim. It is called the *gospel*. (Dr. May asks for permission and recognizes that an animist will have some respect for the Bible already.)

TR: Thank you for your concern for me, my son. May I ask why I should listen to the gospel?

Me: Father, it is a word from the living God. Your culture believes that age has something to say and youth has nothing to say. I am aware that I am younger than you, but the book that I hold is a book from the God who lives forever. If 70 years makes one wise, how wise does eternity make someone? (Dr. May is showing that no matter what age the practitioner is, an eternal God is infinitely wiser.)

TR: That truth is very good, my son; perhaps I need to listen to this book.

Me: Baba, let me begin with a story, a story of a man named Nicodemus. The man in this story is very wise; in fact among the Jewish people of his day, he is the wisest man among them—the chief teacher. This wise man goes by night, however, to Jesus to ask him questions, because he knows that no matter how wise he is, this Jesus is wiser. This Jesus has the words of life; Nicodemus longs to hear these words from this Jesus. (Notice that Dr. May has begun with the story of John 3. You can use this same story.)

TR: Please tell me more of this Jesus.

Me: The story of this Jesus begins at the beginning of the Book. The Book tells us that God created us in His image. He made us to have a relationship with Him. You in your culture know how important relationships are. The story tells of the time in which the man and the woman—the first man and the first woman—were in the garden, a beautiful garden that God had created for them. In that garden God had set one tree and said to them, "Do not eat from this tree; you may eat from every other tree, but if you eat from this tree, you will surely die." The enemy (an evil spirit named Satan) appeared as a serpent and tempted them. They listened to him, they disobeyed the God who was God to them, and they ate from the tree. When they ate, their disobedience brought fear into their lives. They formerly walked with God; now they feared Him. (Dr. May is highlighting how the Creator God brought us into being. He is also discussing the idea of fear.)

TR: I understand this fear. This is the same fear that we feel.

Me: Yes, you see, Father, when we sinned against God back in the beginning, when our fathers sinned against God, that fear affected us all. You know in your tribe how if the chief does something wrong, it affects the whole tribe; so when the first man, Adam, sinned, his sin affected all of us. Therefore, we now live in fear. This fear is caused by sin; sin is so serious that sin must be dealt with. You know that in your culture when people break the rules of the tribe, the tribe must punish that breakage of the rules. (Remember, teaching a lost person the idea of sin is critical.)

TR: Yes, that is true. The tribe cannot allow the rules of the tribe to be violated without dealing with them.

Me: Exactly, or the tribe will not survive.

TR: Please tell me, how did God deal with the breaking of the rules?

Me: The Bible says that the wages of sin is death. All people experienced death—not only physically but also spiritually, Father. Spiritual death is that fear that we all feel; spiritual death is that separation from God that we all experience—that emptiness within. (Dr. May is utilizing Rom. 6:23)

TR: How do I deal with that separation and emptiness? In our tribe we try to go through the ancestors to appease the great god.

Me: Father, the ancestors are people like we are. Even though they are the best of our tribes, still they, too, are sinners as we are. They have no more way to go to God than do we. Their sin does not allow them to enter the presence of God any more than our sin does. Instead, we need someone who can take care of our sins. Long ago a wise chief asked God for a mediator who could lay hold of both God and humanity (Job 9:33).

TR: We, too, know that we need a mediator. Tell me, who is this someone?

Me: Yes, God Himself became this mediator. The God of heaven chose to become a person and lived on this earth. He is this Jesus about whom I spoke. He lived a life without sin and lived in fellowship with the Father. He did not experience the fear that we experience; He did not know the shame we feel. He lived in full fellowship with the Father, yet one day the Bible tells us that evil men took Him and killed Him. (You can use 1 Tim. 2:5 or Rom. 5:8.)

TR: This is terrible; why would they kill a good man?

Me: They killed this man because of their hearts, but God actually sent this man to die—He was killed by God's plan. He was sent to offer Himself as the final ransom payment—the true sacrifice for sin. You know in your culture that when people do wrong, they have to bring a sacrifice to make the thing right. God requires such a sacrifice. When Jesus died, He offered himself as the sacrifice so that sin could be forgiven and that fear could be taken away. In fact God's Book—the Bible—tells us this wonderful truth. Hebrews 2:14-15, NIV says, *Since the children have flesh and blood, He too shared in their humanity so that by His death He might destroy Him who holds the power of death—that is, the devil—and free those who all their lives were held in slav-*

ery by their fear of death. When Jesus died, He paid the price for sin. He defeated the devil, our great enemy. He released us from fear so that we no longer have fear. He rose from the grave. He defeated death and emerged from the grave alive. He is alive today to give real freedom to those who need Him.

TR: Tell me how I find this freedom from fear.

Me: Baba, the way we experience this freedom from fear is to trust Christ. We do this by saying, "You are the only one who can free me from fear. I have sinned against you; my sin shows up in the fear in which I live. I have tried to find a way to you through ancestors, through *Nyangas* (traditional medicine people), and I have not found a way to You, but I believe that Jesus is the way to You. Jesus, I believe You died for me and rose again. I ask you to forgive me of my sin and to take away my fear." Father, if you will confess that Jesus is your Lord, He will forgive you of your sin. He will take away your fear; He will give you the assurance of peace with Him. He will give you true power — power over death and power over your enemy, the devil. This is the Word of God. (Dr. May has given a simple sinner's prayer at the end of a very simple gospel presentation. Remember: do not overcomplicate this task. All the people need to hear is the truth of the gospel.)

(Option 3)

Ebele Adioye is a church planter from the Ivory Coast. After he received his doctorate in missiology in America, he returned to his homeland to become a prolific church planter. I asked Ebele whether he would share his evangelization approach that he uses among North Africans. This approach can be used not only with North Africans but with animists from all over the world. Note how the themes of fear and power dominate the presentation. Also note the simplicity of the presentation itself.

Ebele Adioye wrote the following:[8]

"In Sub-Sahara Africa people struggle for control and power. They fight for dominion over life predicaments and view life as a warfare. A Baoule woman, working three months ago in my farm, throughout the day sang the following maxim: '*La vie est un combat,*' meaning 'Life is a warfare.' African people approach and deal with life from a warfare perspective. In this warfare, peace, joy, salvation, and stability require the intervention of powers and forces greater than what humanity can provide.

"Theodicy in an African context is just a matter of the rapport of force or power. The strongest must win. The omnipotence of God is a divine attribute that surely impresses the African mind. Presenting the gospel in such a context requires some basic contextual effort. I propose *A Spiritual Warfare Gospel Presentation Approach* as an approach that can offer good results in this part of the world."

A WARFARE GOSPEL PRESENTATION OR CONVERSATION

Step One: Raising Questions on the Weakness of Humanity

In presenting the gospel to a typical African person, one should raise the question of human weakness in front of evils. The best question should be: Why are we powerless in front of sorcery, witchcraft, demons, and Satan? The question will receive many answers. The person presenting the gospel will proceed regardless of the answer the respondent gives.

Step Two: Enumerating the Effects of Humanity's Weakness

The gospel-sharer will offer some examples of human sufferings that illustrate the weakness of humanity. A Westerner must understand that what constitutes a weakness of a person in his or her context may differ from what an African woman perceives. Here is a list of life challenges in Africa: sickness, death of babies, death of a young adult, accident, lack of rain, death of a brilliant student, barrenness, dreams (dreams of death, sickness, of sexual relationship with one's mate or even with a different person), divorce, or any other marital conflicts. This list is just an example of what in an African context may constitute a serious life predicament that requires an intervention of power. The gospel-sharer may choose one or two of these life issues and narrate its effects on families, societies, or life in general. The gospel-sharer hereafter will ask the question: What will you do to defeat these evils?

Step Three: Listening to the Propositions of the Prospects

The gospel-sharer must pay a closer attention to the responses of the contact-person (the one you are evangelizing). The contact-person's responses will give valuable information on his or her religious background. The response of the contact-person does not stop the conversation. After listening carefully to the contact-person, the gospel-sharer will propose the next step with the following transitional sentences, "The Bible offers a valuable story that answers this serious question; please let us go through some of them briefly."

Step Four: Narrating Biblical Answers
to the Issue of Humanity's Weakness

The gospel-sharer then will open the Bible to the Book of Genesis and will narrate the story of the fall from a power and weakness perspective (Editor's note: Gen. 1-3). The story goes as follows:

God is the most powerful Being of all time. His power clearly is revealed in the Bible through what He created. He created heaven and earth, stars, moon, and sun. He created angels, water, and creatures living in it. God created all the animals, birds, and people living on the earth. Of all the creatures of God, He gave power to human beings and wanted them to rule and take care of the rest of his creation on earth. But one day the people He created lost their God-given power; the Bible tells us how it happened.

God, the most powerful King, told humanity to rule over what God created; but like Satan, the enemy of God, the people wanted more power. The first man and his wife wanted to be more powerful than God Himself. To achieve their goal they accepted a forbidden fruit that Satan gave them. From that day they lost contact with God; they became powerless; they lost their peace, joy, love; and they became vulnerable to sickness, death, demons, sorcery, and all evil things. The first human being, Adam, became so weak and powerless that he and his family began to seek power, deliverance, protection, and peace in things God created instead of God Himself. So, humanity's disobedience is the cause of its weakness in front of evils.

God did not leave people without help. He provided a wonderful plan to get out of this trouble. First, God rebuked Satan and cursed him. He told Satan that a child would be sent to earth to defeat Satan. This child was the only Son of God. He was sent many years later; His name is *Jesus,* because He was sent to save people from bondage and wickedness of evil. First, He died for humanity's disobedience. He now gives, to anyone who believes in Him, power to become children of God (John 1:12).

Step Five: Proposing Biblical Answers to the Contact Person

Today, if you give Him your heart and life, He not only will give you power of forgiveness by reconciling you with His Father and remove the curse of your disobedience, He also will give you power to become a child of God. He will, thereafter, remove the fear of evils and the evil ones in your heart. He will give you peace; never again will you be a slave to the enemies of God. Will you want to ask Jesus Christ to enter your heart and give you power to become a child of God as well as destroy the work of Satan and the evil one in your life? If you accept that truth, Jesus will do it, because He promised that He was sent to earth to destroy the work of the devil. Do you want Him in your life? (The gospel-sharer then can lead the contact person in prayer.) The gospel-sharer then will take contact information and make an appointment for further biblical stories on the power that helps new Christians grow in grace, love, holiness, and spiritual warfare, etc.

Step Six: Follow-Up Strategy

For a follow-up, the gospel-sharer may invite the contact person to a series of selected Bible stories that help the new believer grow in power. The Bible is full of stories that help believers grow in power: power of prayer, power of the Word of God, power of love, power of faith, power of sanctification, power of the gospel, power of fellowship and Christian communion, etc. The rule is simple: teach in a narrative way.

Note: In Step 5, you might have to describe in greater detail how Christ can give you the power that Ebele Adioye discussed. The reader can use the following verses to further highlight how one can trust God as Savior. For more in-depth discussion of these verses and how to use them, please refer to pages 37-42 in "How to Witness to Your Catholic Friends."

- Romans 3:23—We are all sinners.
- Romans 6:23—Our sin has consequences.
- Romans 5:8—Jesus was sent to be the sacrifice for our sin.
- Romans 10:9—How one can surrender to Christ as Lord
- Romans 10:13—Anyone can surrender his or her life to Christ.

Follow-up Questions/Statements an Animist Might Ask You

1) You don't understand the power I feel when I interact with the Spirit world.

Your response: I don't deny that the spirit world has power. However, the power you feel is not from God. The Bible talks about the power of the demonic. In Ephesians 2:1-3 it says, *And you He made alive, who were dead in trespasses and sins, in which you once walked according to the course of this world, according to the prince of the power of the air, the spirit who now works in the sons of disobedience, among whom also we all once conducted ourselves in the lusts of our flesh, fulfilling the desires of the flesh and of the mind, and were by nature children of wrath, just as the others.*

However, let's examine the purpose of this power. The Bible is very clear on the destructive nature of evil power. John 10:10a says, *"The thief does not come except to steal, and to kill, and to destroy."*

Power can feel good momentarily, but ultimately it is designed to deceive you from the BEST God has for you.

2) Part of my belief is that my ancestors can help me. Do you not believe your ancestors can help you?

(Option 1)

Your response: We believe in heaven are millions of people that have gone before us, who gave their life to Christ before they died, and who are witnesses to what we do. In Hebrews 12:1-2a, NIV, the Bible says, *Therefore, since we are surrounded by such a great cloud of witnesses, let us throw off everything that hinders and the sin that so easily entangles. And let us run with perseverance the race marked out for us, fixing our eyes on Jesus, the pioneer and perfecter of faith.*

You are not alone. You have men and women who have gone before you. However, we believe that our God is all-powerful and all-knowing. If someone is all-powerful, He can help us without the aid of others. Consequently, those ancestors even may be aware of what we are doing, but God of the universe is controlling what is occurring.

In Jeremiah 32:17 the Bible tells us, *"'Ah, Lord GOD! Behold, You have made the heavens and the earth by Your great power and outstretched arm. There is nothing too hard for You.'"*

If nothing is too difficult for Him, when we put our trust in Him, He—not our ancestors—is the one to help us.

(Option 2)
Although our loved ones already have entered eternity, God clearly forbids that we contact our ancestors for guidance. We can remember them fondly and remember how God used them in our lives. However, spirit contact with the dead is dangerous. In fact, we might actually be talking to demons who are lying to us about their true identity.[9]

In Deuteronomy 18:10-14, NIV, the Bible says,

Let no one be found among you who sacrifices their son or daughter in the fire, who practices divination or sorcery, interprets omens, engages in witchcraft, or casts spells, or who is a medium or spiritist or who consults the dead. Anyone who does these things is detestable to the LORD; because of these same detestable practices the LORD your God will drive out those nations before you. You must be blameless before the LORD your God. The nations you will dispossess listen to those who practice sorcery or divination. But as for you, the LORD your God has not permitted you to do so.

In 1 Corinthians 10:19-22, NIV, the Bible says, *Do I mean then that food sacrificed to an idol is anything, or that an idol is anything? No, but the sacrifices of pagans are offered to demons, not to God, and I do not want you to be participants with demons. You cannot drink the cup of the Lord and the cup of demons too; you cannot have a part in both the Lord's table and the table of demons. Are we trying to arouse the Lord's jealousy? Are we stronger than he?*

3) I have my traditions; you have your traditions.
Your response: In Hebrews 10:1-10 the Bible talks about tradition.

For the law, having a shadow of the good things to come, and not the very image of the things, can never with these same sacrifices, which they offer continually year by year, make those who approach perfect. For then would they not have ceased to be offered? For the worshipers, once purified, would have had no more consciousness of sins. But in those sacrifices there is a reminder of sins every year. For it is not possible that the blood of bulls and goats could take away sins. Therefore, when He came into the world, He said:

"Sacrifice and offering You did not desire,
But a body You have prepared for Me.
In burnt offerings and sacrifices for sin
You had no pleasure.
Then I said, 'Behold, I have come—
In the volume of the book it is written of Me—
To do Your will, O God.'"

Previously saying, "Sacrifice and offering, burnt offerings, and offerings for sin You did not desire, nor had pleasure in them" (which are offered according to the

law), then He said, "Behold, I have come to do Your will,
O God." He takes away the first that He may establish the
second. By that will we have been sanctified through the
offering of the body of Jesus Christ once for all.

God is telling his people that priestly sacrifice and the shedding of the blood of animals are not enough to make Him satisfied. This tradition of the Jews, while good, is not satisfactory. Ultimately, traditions might be a good thing, but they don't meet the final requirements of God.

Christianity is not about one country's culture or traditions. Christianity is a recognition that the God of the universe has designed a means to live with Him. That means is through His Son Jesus Christ, regardless of one's country or origins.

4) In the past, giving sacrifices to my people always has helped me.

The Bible says one great God exists. Often He gives us help whether we realize it or not. You have been living under the grace of God. Even as you sacrifice to others, God actually has been the One that has allowed you to be healed or to receive a blessing.

The Bible discusses how in our hearts we all inherently know of the One True God. Romans 1 teaches us that all people, no matter their origin, have known that One True God is in control. This One True God also is in control of your life. In Romans 1:18-32 the Bible says this:

For the wrath of God is revealed from heaven against all
ungodliness and unrighteousness of men, who suppress
the truth in unrighteousness, because what may be known
of God is manifest in them, for God has shown it to them.
For since the creation of the world His invisible attributes
are clearly seen, being understood by the things that are

made, even His eternal power and Godhead, so that they are without excuse, because, although they knew God, they did not glorify Him as God, nor were thankful, but became futile in their thoughts, and their foolish hearts were darkened. Professing to be wise, they became fools, and changed the glory of the incorruptible God into an image made like corruptible man—and birds and four-footed animals and creeping things.

Therefore God also gave them up to uncleanness, in the lusts of their hearts, to dishonor their bodies among themselves, who exchanged the truth of God for the lie, and worshiped and served the creature rather than the Creator, who is blessed forever. Amen.

For this reason God gave them up to vile passions. For even their women exchanged the natural use for what is against nature. Likewise also the men, leaving the natural use of the woman, burned in their lust for one another, men with men committing what is shameful, and receiving in themselves the penalty of their error which was due. And even as they did not like to retain God in their knowledge, God gave them over to a debased mind, to do those things which are not fitting; being filled with all unrighteousness, sexual immorality, wickedness, covetousness, maliciousness; full of envy, murder, strife, deceit, evil-mindedness; they are whisperers, backbiters, haters of God, violent, proud, boasters, inventors of evil things, disobedient to parents, undiscerning, untrustworthy, unloving, unforgiving, unmerciful; who, knowing the righteous judgment of God, that those who practice such things are deserving of death, not only do the same but also approve of those who practice them.

God bless you as your share your faith with your animistic friends. Missionaries around the world have seen great success among these peoples of Africa, South America, and Asia. I pray the same success for you.

[1]*http://www.ijfm.org/PDFs_IJFM/11_2_PDFs/07_Love.pdf.*

[2]Stark, Rodney, *What Americans Really Believe* (Waco: Baylor University Press, 2008), 62-63.

[3]See "Flaw of the Excluded Middle" by Paul Hiebert in *Missiology* 10:1 (January 1982, pp. 35-47).

[4]Bledsoe, David. Email interview (January 2012).

[5]Ibid.

[6]Ibid. The Bledsoe material is a copy of that interview, with slight editorial input of Bledsoe's approach.

[7]May, Stan. Email interview (January 2012).

[8]Adioye, Ebele. Email interview (January 2012).

[9]Bledsoe, David. Email interview (January 2012).

Chapter 6

How to Witness
to Your Muslim Friends

Lately, Islam constantly seems to be in the news. With more than 1.5 billion adherents Islam has become a visible and controversial factor on the world stage.[1] In fact, in many ways, Islam has become THE major religious player. In 2011 the world watched the "Arab Spring" with a mixture of joy (at the hopes of democracies in many Muslim states) and fear (at the concern of what those democracies might bring with these newfound freedoms). With mixed anxieties we continue to watch the continual tensions in the Middle East.

Post 9-11, Muslims in the United States have faced complicated times. For many Muslims, their day-to-day life is focused on simply trying to live a moral life, rear a solid family, and put in a good day's work. At the same time, many of these Muslims are trying to worship their God without interference. However, a believer in Jesus Christ must understand that an Islamic perspective on God, Jesus, Scripture, government, and daily life is profoundly different from that of our own. If people attempt to witness to a Muslim by thinking that they are speaking to a monotheist who views the world similarly to the way a Christian does, they are profoundly mistaken. This chapter will explain a few of those differences.

Believers must walk into a witness with a Muslim with an understanding of who this Muslim is before God. Every Muslim has been *fearfully and wonderfully made* (Ps. 139:14). They are descendants of Abraham and rightly deserve our respect (Gen. 16). They are valuable enough to God that He longs for them to repent and have saving faith in Him (1 Tim. 2:4).

In short, they merit our love and our time.

Where Did Islam Originate?

Mohammed was born in 570 A.D. His father died shortly after his birth. His mother died in 576. Consequently, he lived with his grandfather. As he traveled with his grandfather for commercial purposes, Mohammed more than likely encountered a variety of Jewish and Christian sects in the area.

From 585-590 he was apprenticed by Khadija, a rich widow and Ebionite Christian. Mohammed proved to be a very reliable worker and competent man. By 596 he married Khadija (she was 40 at the time). As he had done very well in life, and as Khadija was a wealthy widow, he was able to spend a great deal of his time in meditation in nearby caves.

By 610 Mohammed received his first vision from someone Muslims claim to be the angel Gabriel. These visions discussed the uselessness of idols and the unity of God. Mohammed, however, was unsure of these visions. He was unsure whether they actually were divine or demonic. Ultimately Khadija and one of his uncles assured Mohammed that these visions were from God. Mohammed began to feel more confident in the visions and began to share the message.

By 613 Mohammed had 13 converts to his preaching; these included his uncle and Khadija. His preaching predominantly was peaceful and was very open to both Jews and Christians. Over time, however, the leaders of Mecca were unhappy with Mohammed and expelled him.[2] By 619 Khadija and Mohammed's uncle died. Mohammed then married several other women including A'isha, a 7-year old (unconsummated until she was 9).

In 622 Mohammed fled to Medina after an attack on his life. Muslims count this date as the beginning of the religion. In 624 Mohammed began a military offensive; his small army defeated a much larger force of Meccans in Badr. By 630 Mohammed's force had conquered all of Arabia. Mohammed died in 632.

Islam's incredible rate of growth occurred after Mohammed's death. Before the onset of Islam, Arabians were known as fierce fighters. However, Arabians never fought in a unified manner. With the advent of Islam, Arabs preceded to defeat two dominant world powers—the Persian Empire to the East and the Byzantine Empire to the West. From there, Islam basically spread from Iran to Southern Europe in a span of about 80 years. What began as a religion from the deserts of the Arabian peninsula became a cohesive world empire that has lasted for 1,300 years.

The Belief System

The strength of Islam is in its simplicity. Every Christian should understand the core principles behind Islam. Islam is based on submission to the one true god.[3] The very word *Islam* means submission. In the Koran, his one true god is defined by 99 names. Whereas Christianity maintains that a personal relationship exists between God and man, in Islam Allah is unknowable. In Islam the very idea of a personal relationship with Allah is not taught.

Core Practices of Islam

Islam has five pillars of belief. A practicing Muslim participates in the following activities:

1) Confession—On a daily basis a Muslim will be heard to say, "I declare there is no god but Allah and Mohammed is his prophet." In fact, recitation of this phrase is tantamount to conversion to Islam.

2) Salat — Prayer five times daily facing Mecca. Initially, Muslims faced Jerusalem, but after repeated rejection by the Jews, Mohammed changed his prayer direction toward Mecca.

3) Zakat — Charitable giving of 1/40th of the adherent's income. (Before you decide that this is an easy amount compared to the Christian tithe, remember that in 2008 the average charitable donation of churchgoers was less than 2.5 percent, or 1/40th, annually!)

4) Ramadan — During the month of Ramadan, Muslims fast. During this time period between sunrise and sunset Muslims do not eat, smoke, drink any liquids, or have sexual intercourse. Small children, the elderly, soldiers, and pregnant women are exempt from this duty.

5) Hajj — At least once in their lives all Muslims who are financially able make a journey to Mecca.

These five pillars make up the daily practice of Muslims. This simple system of adherence makes the entire religion quite easy for the average person to follow.

Core Beliefs of Islam

Islam's belief system centers on five major themes.

1) Allah — The creator of the universe. Allah is good but unknowable. The Islamic view unquestionably is monotheistic.

2) Prophets — A strong overlap exists between Islam and Christianity. Muslims believe in Adam, Noah, Abraham, David, and Jesus as prophets. However, Mohammed is the last and ultimate prophet.

3) Angels and spirits — God's creation contains good angels and bad angels. All Muslims have a guardian angel and two recording angels. However, negative angels called *jinn* also exist; they can cause trouble here on earth. Many folk Muslims seek to manipulate the *jinn* for their own purposes. (See the chapter on animism to understand the use of spirits and manipulation.)

4) Books—Muslims revere certain books. They believe that the (Zabin) Psalms of David are holy, as are the Torah of Moses and the Gospels (Injil) of Jesus. However, they believe that Christians have corrupted these books and that the ultimate revelation from God, the Koran, is the last and most important Scripture for humanity.

5) Day of Judgment—God ultimately will judge all people. Those that have been faithful to Allah will receive Paradise.

6) Providence—Whatever Allah wills happens. Muslims hold highly to the sovereignty of God.[4]

Muslims, just as Christians do, display varying degrees of commitment to their ideals. As you witness to a Muslim, you might be dealing with someone that holds fervently to all of these beliefs. You might, however, be interacting with someone who has a very low commitment level to what is listed above. Remember, your understanding of these elements of the Muslim faith will, at a minimum, gain you some respect from your Muslim friend. When you demonstrate their belief system is important enough to merit study, this communicates love and friendship.

How does a Christian bridge the gap and begin to witness to his Muslim friends? With Islam, as with the other religions, you can find a variety of ways to approach a discussion about faith.

How to Share Your Faith with a Muslim

(Option 1)

Dr. Wade Akins has been a missionary to Vietnam and Brazil. For the past 16 years he also has been a global trainer in evangelism. Akins has trained more than 20,000 church planters; this typically has occurred in small groups in countries antagonistic to the gospel. He has extensive experience with Muslims and has written a practical work entitled *How to Share Your Faith with Muslims*. I asked Dr. Akins for some sample conversations in dealing with Muslims.[5]

Note the following things as you read his approach to reaching Muslims.

a) In scenario one Akins recognized that his opening conversation was a bridge to the gospel. He knew that typically more than a five-minute presentation is necessary to lead a Muslim to Christ. He used an informal, personal approach to get the person to participate in a quick, evangelistic Bible study. This study, "The Good News of Jesus", takes the reader and leader step-by-step through the life of Christ. Akins mentioned the site on which you can download this study for free. I have used this study many, many times with many adherents from a variety of religious backgrounds and personally can attest to how God seems to use it. I advise you to download this free study from the website *pioneermissions.org*.

b) In scenario two note Akins' simple approach to a cultural Muslim. This is a Muslim who only culturally practices his faith and is not devout. Note the bridge to the gospel and then how he uses the same gospel plan that we used for nominal Catholics or Protestants.

c) In scenario three Akins tells the Muslim that he has read part of the Koran. I strongly encourage you to have read these key chapters that Akins highlights. They do not take long; to have read the Muslim holy book will show great respect for your Muslim friend. You can find English versions of the Koran throughout the Internet as a free download.

WITNESSING TO MUSLIMS
By Wade Akins

Two fundamental keys to witnessing to Muslims exist. One is the Holy Spirit.

Of course, the Holy Spirit plays the key role in every conversion, but this needs to be strongly emphasized when you witness to Muslims. The reason is that one easily can fall into a trap of trying to reason or to argue a Muslim into the faith. This never has happened and never will.

The second key is the Word of God. To be effective one must be able to get the Muslim to at least look at what the Word of God says about sin and salvation.

Since Muslims have no concept of original sin, their entire concept of sin is not one that we as Christians believe from a biblical perspective. They see no need for an atoning, sacrificial death of Christ on the cross. In fact, they do not even believe that Jesus physically died on a cross. The challenge is great!

When I am witnessing to a Muslim, I first try to assess the person's personal commitment to Islam. This will determine which bridge I will use to get the Muslim to look into the Word of God. Again, the key is to get the individual into the Word of God and to let God's Holy Spirit use the Word to convict of sin, righteousness, and judgment.

From my perspective I see Muslims at one of three levels of commitment. I will address each one of these.

First is the level in which your friend is a Muslim by birth but has no commitment at all to Islam. This friend does not even believe in the god Allah or Muhammad. Second is the Muslim that is a cultural Muslim that does believe in Allah and Muhammad but has no idea why and has no understanding of Islamic beliefs or precepts. Third is the committed Muslim who believes in Allah and Muhammad; this person knows the Muslim religion and beliefs very well.

Scenario One: The Muslim who is a Muslim by birth but has no commitment to Islam

While I was in an African nation, I went on a witnessing visit with another believer who never before had been out to evangelize. At one house we met some boys in the yard.

I asked, "Are your parents home?"

"Yes," was the reply.

We went inside and met the man of the house. He invited us to sit down; we introduced ourselves.

After talking about his family and telling them about mine I asked, "May I ask you a spiritual question?"

"Yes," he replied.

"What do you believe about God?," I asked.

His response was, "I do believe that there is a God." That basically was all he knew.

I then asked, "Would you like to know God personally?"

"Yes," he answered.

Then I asked, "May I share a story with you about God?"

Again, he responded, "Yes, I would like that."

I began, "I would like to tell you a story that shares how much God loves you. God created the heavens, the sun, the stars, the moon, and you. He knows the numbers of hairs on your head; He knows your name. And He loves you.

Then I share with him Lesson One from a booklet entitled "The Good News of Jesus" by Christy Brawner. One can download this series of evangelistic Bible studies for free from our web site, *www.pioneermissions.org*.

The lesson has three parts. Part One of Lesson One tells the story of the birth of Jesus from the Book of Matthew. Part Two contains oral questions that review the story. Part Three gives the spiritual truths one learns from the story.

The last spiritual truth of Lesson One says that Jesus Christ is the Emmanuel, God with us!

So, when I completed the entire lesson and shared this last spiritual truth, I looked at the man to see his response. He was very positive. (The truth that Jesus was/is actually God Who lived among us sank in with him.)

I proceeded to go ahead and share the rest of the story about how Christ lived a sinless life but died on a cross. I explained that Christ died in our place and rose from the dead. Then I explained that Christ would forgive him of his sins, write his name in the Book of Life, and put the Holy Spirit into this life. I shared that if he desired, he could call on Christ by faith to enter into his life right now.

He responded by saying, "Yes, that is what I want to do."

I then led him into a simple prayer in which he invited Christ into his life.

The result: He now is attending the nearby church and having weekly Bible studies with his entire family and friends.

Scenario Two: The Muslim who is a cultural Muslim

This friend does believe in Allah and Muhammad but has no idea why and has no understanding of the Islamic beliefs or precepts. My main objective is, as soon as I can, to get this person into the Word of God. I will do this simply by offering a New Testament or Bible.

I simply say, "I have a love gift for you." Then I watch the facial reaction. (In Islam the concepts of *love* and *forgiveness* are foreign, so I like to use these terms when I speak to Muslims.)

My objective simply is to get Muslims to receive God's Word. They may read it at night in secret or openly.

If possible one could say, "May I show you a few verses that explain to you how you may know for sure you will go to Paradise after you die?" If the response is, "Yes," then you share with them either the "Good News of Jesus" (previously mentioned) or the following verses that explain the gospel: 1 John 5:13 and Romans 3:23, 6:23, 5:8, 10:9, and 10:13.

Scenario Three: Committed Muslims who believe in Allah and Muhammad. These Muslims know their religion and beliefs very well.

Editor's Note: Christians need not be intimidated by a Muslim's commitment to his or her faith. Muslims generally are very open to discussing their faith. They aren't always ready to convert, but typically they will give you a hearing. Religion permeates the committed Muslim's life. Discussions of faith are very much a part of this person. To share with this type of Muslim takes a little time; read through the biblical and Koranic passages listed below.

First, I would say, "I have been reading the Koran and have a few questions I would like to ask you." This always creates attention, because Muslims will be surprised to hear that you have been reading their Holy Book.

Ask whether the person could meet you for some time to look at some things from your Scriptures and from his or hers.

If the friend responds by saying, "yes," then when you meet, show the trail of innocent blood for sin in the Bible. This might take several meetings. Use the following passages that overlap in both Holy Books:

1. Describe Creation: Koran 10:1-8; then study Genesis 1.

2. Describe the Fall of Satan: Koran 7:1-18; then study Ezekiel 28:12-16 and Isaiah 14:12-16.

3. Look at Adam and Eve: Koran 2:34-39, 7:11-30. Study Genesis 3; show how Adam and Eve killed an innocent animal to cover themselves. Then show them Koran 20:74 and Romans 3:23. Explain how both say sin results in death. Ask the following question: Do you see how innocent blood was shed because they sinned?

4. Discuss the story of Abraham: Koran 16:1-20 and in the Bible Genesis 22.[6] Study both texts and show how God required innocent blood to be shed for sin. Islam observes a Feast of Id that is a remembrance of Abraham killing an animal as a sacrifice for sin. Ask this question: Do you see how God requires innocent blood to be shed for sin?

5. Examine the story of Jesus: study what the Koran says about Jesus Christ. Observe what the Koran teaches. Turn to *Sura* 3 in your friend's Koran. (I suggest that you buy a Koran in English as well). This chapter talks extensively about Christ. Read *Sura* 3:45-47.

[3.45] (And remember) when the angels said: O Mary! Lo! Allah giveth thee glad tidings of a word from him, whose name is the Messiah, Jesus, son of Mary, illustrious in the world and the Hereafter, and one of those brought near (unto Allah).

[3.46] He will speak unto mankind in his cradle and in his manhood, and he is of the righteous.

[3.47] She said: My Lord! How can I have a child when no mortal hath touched me? He said: So (it will be). Allah createth what He will. If he decreeth a thing. He saith unto it only: Be! And it is.[7]

A. Read in the Koran 3:45—Jesus is the Word of God. Then explain what this means by showing John 1:1 and 1:14.

B. Read in the Koran 3:45—Jesus is the Messiah. Ask, "What does this mean to you"? Answer: "The anointed One."

C. Explain Koran 3:45—Jesus is held in honor.

D. Explain Koran 3:45—Jesus is nearest to Allah. Explain that this means that He knows the way to God and to Paradise. Explain that the words of Jesus are in the Bible; get your friend into the Word of God. Share John 17:3 that explains that Jesus is Eternal Life. Koran 3:46—He is righteous. He knew no sin.

E. Explain Koran 3:47—Jesus was born with no earthly father. Explain why He did not inherit a sinful nature and thus was sinless.

You have just shown that Jesus is the Word of God, is the Messiah, is held in honor, is nearest to Allah, and that He knows the way to Paradise. In the Koran Jesus is special. Take this opportunity to share why Jesus died on a cross. Remember, from birth Muslims are taught that He did not die at all.

Ask: "I know that is what you may not believe that Jesus died on a cross, but may I show you what we believe as Christ followers and why?"

If your friend says, "Yes," then explain the gospel.

Again, feel free to use the studies from the "Good News of Jesus" by Christy Brawner or the six verses that explain the gospel as presented in Scenario Two.

Another Option for Evangelizing Muslims

One of my colleagues who serves in the Middle East agreed to provide a sample conversation he might have with a typical

Muslim.[8] As you read, note:

a) He is highly complimentary of the positive aspects of Islam.

b) He treats his colleague with respect.

c) He doesn't shy away from sharing the differences between the two religions. Unlike non-Christians of the West, most Muslims are VERY open to discussing religion. Faith is not an offensive topic, especially if you don't enter the discussion aggressively.

d) As a Christian he mentions praying throughout the day. Begin this pattern in your life as well. You can approach a Muslim with much more confidence. However, keep that attitude of praying as you go.

e) He mentions Ramadan. For a Muslim this is the month of fasting. If need be, have you considered trying to fast during the day for a few days this year so that you might empathize with your Muslim friend?

Here is my friend's sample conversation which you could pattern when you share your faith.

You: Hello, Ahmed! Peace to you.

Ahmed: And peace to you! How is your family?

You: My family is well. Praise God! And how is your family?

Ahmed: Praise God—all is good!

You: Ahmed, I know that you are a very religious man and that you have a high respect for God.

Ahmed: I do love God very much. As Muslims we are taught to live our whole lives for God. We pray five times each day, give alms to the poor, fast during the month of Ramadan, and read God's holy book. If at all possible, we also make a religious trip to Mecca during our lifetimes.

You: I have to admit that this is quite a list. I think I would have a difficult time living up to all the requirements in Islam. Last year the weather was really hot during Ramadan. I think I would have been tempted to drink something during the day. And five prayer times each day seems like a lot. On many days I think I would have a tough time stopping what I am doing to make time for the ritual washings (ablutions) and go through the prayers I have seen being made by devout Muslim men. This seems like a fairly involved process. Personally I love to pray and try to do so every day but am afraid that I would not always be able to live up to the requirements in Islam. How about you, Ahmed? Are you always able to live up to the requirements of praying five times each day?

Ahmed: Fasting is difficult during the years when Ramadan is during the hot season. I have two friends who have difficult jobs in the heat. Sometimes they give in and take a drink of water in the middle of the day. To be honest some days I do miss a couple of prayer times when I am in the middle of a job I can't stop.

You: But this is OK—right?

Ahmed: Not really. We are required by Islam to fulfill all the requirements of Islam. This is why Islam is the best and true religion.

You: Oh, I see!

Ahmed: How many times a day do you pray?

You: Well, I don't really know. I pray all day long. I just pray as I go through the day.

Ahmed: I have heard this about Christians. To me this seems strange. As I understand it, you don't really have any rules about your prayers. You don't face in a certain direction or have certain times for prayer. You don't even have certain prayers for different prayer times. How can this be?

You: I see how this could seem really strange, but you are

correct in everything you have said. I pray any place and at any time. I can pray right now while I am talking to you. As a matter of fact during this conversation I already have prayed a couple of times that God would bless our time together and that He would bless both of us.

Ahmed: How can you believe you are prepared to pray when you have not washed the dirt from your body?

You: That is a great question. In Matthew 23 Jesus deals with the question. He indicates that the outside of the body is not what makes a person acceptable to God but rather the condition of that person's heart. In fact, Ahmed, this is a common theme of the entire Bible. I believe God cares much more about the spiritual condition of my heart than He does about the appearance of cleanliness or religiosity on the outside. Therefore, since God is everywhere, as long as my heart is in a right condition, I am able to talk to God and He is able to talk to me.

Ahmed: Wait a minute! You are saying that God talks to you? How can this be? God is great; you are just a person! In our religion this is a blasphemous idea.

You: I know it is; I don't mean to offend. But I simply have such a close relationship with God that I like to share this with people I know and love. My relationship with God is the best part of my life; I want my friends to know that.

Ahmed: Praise God! Praise God! God is great! But all of this seems so foreign to me. How can you be so perfect in your religion that you could have a relationship with God? Islam teaches that this is impossible. And you seem to be admitting that you don't do all the religious things that God requires, yet you claim to have a relationship with Him. How can this be?

You: This is a great question and one I want to answer, but let's save it for a little bit later in our discussion. I think we could look at something that will help the answer to make more sense. Would this be all right with you?

Ahmed: This is all right with me if God wills.

You: Ahmed, I want to ask you some personal questions. Is that all right as well?

Ahmed: If God wills.

You: Ahmed, does religion answer all of your deepest questions and meet all of your deepest needs?

Ahmed: Islam is the perfect religion. Islam is all that a person needs!

You: All right, let me ask the question this way. When you lay your head down at night and you are alone in the dark, are you at peace? Furthermore, are you at peace when you consider where you will spend eternity?

Ahmed: Eternity is in God's hands. Even Mohammed said that he did not know whether he would go to heaven when he died.

You: That is exactly what I am talking about!

Ahmed: What do you mean?

You: No one ever lived Islam better than Mohammed. Is that true?

Ahmed: Of course!

You: You have admitted that Islam requires some things that you have failed to follow.

Ahmed: That is also true.

You: Then how can you have peace? You seem to believe your status with God and your eternity is uncertain. And nothing robs us of peace more than uncertainty does.

Ahmed: What is your point?

You: I believe God has given us a way to have perfect peace both in this life and about where we will spend eternity. Understanding this way, however, requires an entirely different way of looking at God and religion.

Ahmed: This is where you are going to try and convert me to Christianity. I have to tell you that I have known many Christians.

Many of my best friends are Christians. Their lives are no better than mine.

You: That is why I told you that to understand the way would require a different way of looking at God and religion. I really am not interested in trying to convert you to the Christian religion. However, I am interested in telling you how I began to have a relationship with God.

When I was (use the age you got saved), I realized that I was separated from God. I was doing everything I knew to do through religion to make myself acceptable to God. But when I was alone with my thoughts, I knew that my religion was not sufficient to make me acceptable to God. As you do, I knew that religion required a lot of things of me that I simply could not live up to. I began to understand that my problem was my sin. Sin is an offense to God; nothing I did seemed to take away my awareness of my guilt or to bring me close to God. Then someone told me that I was going at all of this all wrong. This person explained to me that for people to work their way to God through any religion regardless of how sincere they are or how diligently they try is impossible. This person explained that God lived among us by sending Jesus to die as our substitute and that on the cross He paid for my sins. Three days later Jesus arose from the grave to conquer Satan, sin, and death.

Ahmed: The Quran tells us that Jesus did not die on the cross.

You: I realize this, Ahmed. I simply request that you graciously listen to me for a few more minutes. Believe me; I am not trying to offend your heritage or to question your honor or sincerity. However, I want you to understand that the separation that existed between God and me was immediately and forever removed and my shame was replaced with honor and peace the moment I began to believe in what Jesus did for me on the cross. Ahmed, you can have a relationship like this with Jesus. Jesus preached a message of *repentance*. This is a familiar word in

Islam, is it not?

Ahmed: It is.

You: Then you understand that *repentance* means to turn away from something and to move to another. Ahmed, I believe the secret for you to find everything you have been looking and longing for in religion is to turn from religion as your answer and to turn to Jesus and what He did for you on the cross as the answer to all of life's problems and questions. Ahmed, if you will do this, today you will find peace and will also enter into a relationship with God through His Son, Jesus. That relationship will last forever. Would you like to trust in Jesus right now?

Questions/Debates Your Muslim Friend Might Have for You

1) You believe in three Gods; we believe in only one God.

Your response: Christians do not believe in three Gods. We believe in only one God. The Bible is clear that only one God exists (Deut. 6:4-6; Eph. 4:4-6; Isa. 45:5-6). We believe that the one God is so powerful—so unlike us—that He can manifest as the Trinity. In other words Jesus is God, the Holy Spirit is God, and God the Father is God. Each of them has three separate personhoods, but are all one and the same. You and I are not God. We never can be three in one at the same time. He is not one God with three heads. He is one God that works together as three separate persons. Christians believe God is this way as a continual reminder that we never can be as powerful or as perfect as He is.

2) I cannot believe in a God that had sex with Mary to produce Jesus.

Your response: The Bible does not teach that God had sex with Mary. The Bible teaches that Mary was a virgin and that the Holy Spirit implanted Jesus within her. No sexual union occurred between God and Mary. Christians are repulsed by that idea.

3) Muslims are much more devout than Christians are, so we must be correct.

Your response: I'm not sure that Muslims are more devout than Christians are. I know many, many believers who place all of their wealth, time, and energy into the kingdom of God. Muslims are supposed to give 1/40 of their income. Christians are supposed to give at least 10 percent with the idea that ALL of our money is God's. Muslim pray five times daily. Devout Christians are taught to stay in an attitude of prayer all day long (1 Thess. 5:17).

Besides, 1.5 billion Muslims are in the world today. In many Muslim countries, as the call to prayer goes out, can you honestly say that most Muslims stop to pray during the day? This discrepancy is the same with Christianity; many people claim to be Christians but do not live their lives as they should.

4) Muslims look on TV and see the sex and the violence that are portrayed by Christianity. We do not want any religion that has to do with those types of sins.

Your response: You have a very good point about TV. What Hollywood produces and calls *entertainment* repulses true Christians in America. In truth, Hollywood often has nothing to do with Christianity. A majority of people that produce films are not Christians.

Do Christians permit these films to occur? Christians in America cannot control whether someone produces a bad film. A key element in America is FREEDOM. Politically, we are free to choose to follow God or not. Many times when you watch TV, you are watching people who have REJECTED God and certainly are not Christians. They even might claim to be Christians, but the Bible teaches us that we can tell someone is a believer by how the person acts (Mt. 7:15-23).

5) I do not believe that we were born evil. I believe that we need to live our lives under the will of Allah and he will sort everything out.

Your response: Are you a parent? Do you teach a child to lie or be rebellious? Children inherently know how to do WRONG and must be taught how to do RIGHT. How do they know to do wrong? They know because they have been born with a sin nature. God allows us to be born into sin because He wants us to have two glorious gifts. The first of these gifts is freedom. This is the freedom to choose to love Him or not. God does not force anyone to love Him. He wants our unconditional love and commitment. That occurs only as He gives us the freedom to choose to commit to Him. The second gift He wants us to have is the gift of grace. Only when we realize how far short we are to His perfection can we truly appreciate the GIFT it is to know Him. We know Him in our sin because He first loved us. The toughest part of surrendering our lives to God is recognizing that we fall short of His perfect plan. Realizing our sin occurs only when we get rid of our own pride.

6) I do not want to give my life to Jesus because it would dishonor my family members and their traditions.

Your response: I am aware that following Christ will be a difficult decision. After all, people do not want to dishonor their families. God, however, will give you honor if you choose to follow His plan and not your own.

Someone has to be the first person in a family to take a step of faith toward the Truth of Christ. After that person, God works on the hearts of other individuals in your family. For example, Christianity is not a Western religion. My ancestors are from (place your country of origin here). Years ago a missionary had to go to my family/people and tell them about Jesus. Someone had to be the first to accept the message of Christ. Now, many people from my family/people have turned to Him. You might have to be the first in your family.

7) How can I follow a religion that was involved in the Crusades against my people?

Your response: I do not try to defend the Crusades. Nor do I try to attack Muslims for the conquests of former Christian lands in Africa and the Middle East. This was a dark time in both of our religions. These examples reflect how a few people, in a short period of time, can bring dishonor to an entire people for generations. God loves everybody in the world. He does not care whether a person is from Saudi Arabia or the United States. The Crusades do not show the love of God from either side.

8) Your Bible has been corrupted. Our Koran is perfect.

Your response: Our Bible has not been corrupted. Thousands and thousands of scholars have spent their lifetimes studying this Book. In the end the Bible contains the same set of books it always has had. No changes from the Greek and Hebrew, the original languages of the Bible, have occurred.

Sometimes the Bible has different translations in English but not because the words or basic meaning of the Bible has changed at all. Different words might be used, but this happens only because language changes over time, not because the meaning is different. For example, if I were going to translate from English to Farsi or Arabic, I would have to find the proper translation for those people. The same meaning and definitions are the same, but different words to communicate properly are used. The original languages of the Bible—Greek, Hebrew, and Aramaic—have not changed.

9) Christians cannot even get along. You have so many denominations. How can you be right?

Your response: Our denominations do not mean we are divided. If you ask a Presbyterian whether a Baptist is a brother or sister in Christ, the answer will be YES. However, we may have differences of opinion on worship styles and lesser issues of Scripture. Just as God has made different types of people with different preferences, He allows us to have different ways to worship Him. Christians agree on the fundamentals of the faith—the fact that the Bible is God's Word, that Jesus is Lord, that Christ will return, and the Trinity. Besides, do Muslims not have divisions? Do all Shi'ites agree with all Sunnis? Do all Persians agree with all Arabs? I think not.

May God bless you as you respond to these questions and attempt to share your faith with your Muslim friends.

[1]*http://www.adherents.com/Religions_By_Adherents.html* (accessed 11-7-2011).

[2]Special thanks to both Dr. Stan May and Dr. Wade Akins for their background information from both lecture notes and from Dr. Akins' book, *How to Share Your Faith with Muslims*.

[3]*God* is written as *god* instead of being capitalized. The One True God in which Christians believe is a Trinitarian God. God the Father, Son, and the Holy Spirit all are persons of the One True God. God is a single Being that is comprised of three Persons. The Muslim god does not recognize Jesus nor the Holy Spirit as part of the Trinity. Therefore, by the very definition of the Christian God, the Muslim description of God does not fit into our paradigm. Christians and Muslims do NOT worship the same God. However, for language clarification, using the term *Allah* for *God* when you witness to Muslims certainly is acceptable—even with the differences in meaning. In Arabic *Allah* simply means *god*. In a later conversation with your friend you can discuss the nuances in meaning.

[4]Corduan, Winfried, *Neighboring Faiths* (Downers Grove, IL: Intervarsity Press, 1998). In the above sections also special thanks to Dr. Stan May and his class notes.

[5]Muslims believe that Ishmael rather than Isaac was on the altar. On this point the Christian would be wise to "agree to disagree".

[6]*The Glorious Koran: A Bilingual Edition with English Translation, Introduction and Notes*, translated by Marmaduke Pickthall (Albany: State University of New York Press, 1976), 69.

[7]For security reasons the name of the author of this section has been withheld. However, in his particular country he is one of the longest-tenured missionaries from his missions organization; he has extensive experience in sharing his faith.

Chapter 7

How to Witness
to Your Buddhist Friends

Buddhism is one of the fastest-growing faiths in the United States today. Buddhism's appeal is far-ranging and strikes a chord at many people's desire for freedom from organized religion.

The type of Buddhism a person practices typically depends on the area of the world from which the person hails. When people are from Japan, they might practice Sokka Gakkai or even Zen Buddhism. Those from Laos or Thailand will practice Theravada Buddhism. Your friends from China are more likely to practice Mahayana or Tibetan Buddhism.

Why is Buddhism becoming so popular in the West and in the United States in particular? A multitude of factors contribute to Buddhism's popularity. Most Westerners are completely unaware of the subsets of the Buddhist faith. Consequently, people of the West can pick and choose positives of each belief system within Buddhism to fit their own needs while they never actually understand the intricacies of what their practiced branch of Buddhism teaches. Tibetan Buddhism interests Americans because of the very congenial Dalai Lama as well as because of our natural sympathy toward the nation of Tibet in the midst of Chinese persecution. Theravada Buddhism (Southeast Asian Buddhism) evokes interest among Westerners because of the apparent sincerity of the monks who practice this faith. These monks genuinely believe in what they are doing and act on these beliefs by leading fervent lives of prayer. Mahayana Buddhism attracts

Westerners because it stresses being "open-minded" and accepting. Finally, Zen Buddhism has a "chic" appeal for those who are seeking to find relaxation in this world. For example, Westerners assume if legendary pro basketball coach Phil Jackson can figure out a way to deal with Kobe Bryant AND Shaquille O'Neal, and he's a Buddhist, Jackson must have some secret that we could use. In other words, MOST Westerners with whom I have conversed about Buddhism are interested in the faith in general but are unaware of its specific teachings.

Background of Buddhism

Buddhism is an offshoot of Hinduism. Both of these world religions were birthed in India. Buddhism was a reaction to the exclusivism of Hinduism. In Hinduism, with the caste system of India, the only ones who truly have a chance at eternal bliss are those who happened to be born in the right caste.[1] For some devout young men this focus on caste proved unsatisfactory.

Buddhism began with a young prince named Siddhartha Gautama (563-483 B.C.). Gautama lived a privileged but sheltered life. His family tried to shield him from the rigors of the outside world. One day, at around age 30, Gautama went outside the confines of his palatial dwelling and saw four unnerving sights. He saw an old man, a deceased body, a beggar, and a calm ascetic. These sights revealed to him the difficulties of life; he immediately renounced everything he had (including a wife and child, but at a later date the wife became a follower).

Gautama's purpose in life was to determine a way to leave the suffering of this life (called *samsara*). He sought a life of great asceticism. He soon garnered some followers because of his adherence to the ascetic ideal.

Gautama was entirely devoted to his plight of finding enlightenment. Tradition states that Gautama often lived on one grain of rice per day. One day, while he was sitting under a Bodhi tree,

111

he had a revelation. This moment of "enlightenment" proved pivotal to Gautama. He realized that he could find a middle path between asceticism and living life opulently.

Gautama immediately ate, felt better, and told his followers about his revelation. Needless to say, they were not pleased. After all, they had committed themselves to the ideals of asceticism. Their leader now was explaining that the sacrifices they had made were not leading them to enlightenment. Eventually, Gautama (who became known as Gautama Buddha, with *Buddha* meaning "enlightened one") persuaded his followers that the middle path was the correct manner to live.

Buddha began to attract more and more followers. As with Christianity, at its foundation Buddhism is a missionary religion.[2] Buddha began to teach his followers the truths he had attained. This teaching became known as the *dharma*.[3] His followers wrote down the *dharma*; it began to be known as the Buddhist scriptures called the *Tripitaka*. Thus Buddhism was born.

What Buddhists Believe

The foundation of Buddhism is represented by the four noble truths. These truths are as follows:

1) To live is to suffer.
2) Suffering is caused by desire.
3) One can eliminate suffering if one eliminates desire.
4) Desire is eliminated by using the Eightfold Path.

The first three aspects are somewhat self-explanatory. First, in life we have suffering. Buddhists recognize the obvious fact that this world consists of a great deal of pain. The notion of suffering is not intended to be pessimistic. Instead, for the Buddhist, this gives a "pragmatic perspective" to a broken world and is the first step in an attempt to rectify it.[4] Second, all suffering is caused by desire. Third, if Buddhists can eliminate desires from their lives, they will eliminate suffering. Consequently, we can eliminate the pain we have in this world and eventually will reach Nirvana—the absolute absence of suffering.

Finally, how does a Buddhist go about fulfilling the fourth truth and eliminate desire? A Buddhist must follow the Eightfold Path. Depending on the source, the Eightfold Path can have different wordings, but it reads as:

1) Right view
2) Right speech
3) Right intention
4) Right action
5) Right livelihood
6) Right effort
7) Right concentration
8) Right mindfulness

If adherents follow these steps, they can eliminate desire from their lives and can end the cycle of suffering. Once they end the cycle of suffering, they are ready to experience Nirvana. If they do not reach perfection in this life, they can continue on the cycle of reincarnation to attempt Nirvana again on the next cycle. As with Hinduism, an adherent has to deal with the karma of this life. If Buddhists do something wrong, they will experience negative consequences on the journey toward Nirvana. If they do something good, this always brings positive consequences. For the Christian the idea of complete and immediate forgiveness of sins is a fundamental aspect of the faith. For the Buddhist the idea of complete forgiveness for sin (except on attainment of Nirvana) primarily is a foreign concept.

In theory the foundations of Buddhism really are quite simple. In practice Buddhism is far more complicated. Dr. Stan May stated, "People accuse Christianity of being a religion based on works. They assume Buddhism lets you do whatever you want. In practice Buddhism is far more works-based than Christianity. If people want to follow Buddhism because they think it's an easy path, they don't know Buddhism."[5]

Buddhism also has split into many splinter groups. It has two primary groups: Theravada and Mahayana. One other group has reached such prominence in the Western worldview that it is included as well.

1) Theravada Buddhism — This is the most conservative of all the Buddhist groups and is found in Southeast Asia and Sri Lanka. Textbooks teach that Buddha is just a person and is not considered a deity in this branch of Buddhism. However, unofficially millions of adherents worship Buddha as divine. This type of Buddhism is centered on personal action such as becoming a monk or meditating. Ultimately, in this branch of Buddhism one must become a monk to reach Nirvana.

2) Mahayana Buddhism — This is the more "liberal" branch of Buddhism. The idea of reaching Nirvana is more open to the common individual. Many Buddhas — not only just Gautama Buddha — may exist. This branch introduced the idea of the Bodhisattva. These are individuals who have died and could have attained Nirvana but have chosen to stay in this realm to help individuals also attain enlightenment.

3) Zen Buddhism — Typically Zen Buddhism would not be included on this list. Instead, Tibetan Buddhism typically would be considered the third prominent branch of Buddhism. However, Zen is the Japanese form of Buddhism that has become popular in the West. This group centers its belief on mediation as well. One can attain enlightenment by entering a meditative state. A person can focus on an object or an unanswerable question such as "What is the sound of one hand clapping?" Once one realizes that the question is not the issue and that the answer is irrelevant, you have taken a step closer to enlightenment.[6]

Final Thoughts

Buddhism is remarkably broad. Understanding these broad concepts as well as its most common practices is important. Familiarity with someone's belief system shows that you RESPECT and HONOR that person.

Before you think that you don't know enough about Buddhism to engage a practicing Buddhist in a meaningful conversation, remember this truth: Most Buddhists will not know the majority of the facts stated above. They are Buddhists because they were born that way, not because they practice the intricacies of this religion.[7] When you witness to Buddhists, the conversations that follow will give you an open door, but along the way you will have to expect many more conversations.

How to Explain Your Faith to Your Buddhist Friends

Follow the first four steps that have been highlighted in other chapters. If you want a thorough overview of the next four steps, please review pages 33-37. The four steps are:

Step 1—Befriend them.
Step 2—Avoid the urge to **just** be their friend and never engage in a spiritual conversation.
Step 3—Look for spiritual clues.
Step 4—Seize the initiative, even if spiritual clues do not present themselves.

These four steps can be applied to all religions. Because Buddhism is diverse, at this point you have several options about how to proceed. This first option deals with a Buddhist's dilemma of never being able to attain Nirvana. While he worked overseas, Jay, a church multiplication trainer in Southeast Asia, learned a new approach to evangelism. A lawyer in the country in which he serves taught him a different approach to speak to Buddhists. This method, now called the "Lawyer's Method", has seen great success among Buddhists in his country.[8] In fact, in the last two years more than 8,500 Buddhists have trusted Christ.

As you read the "Lawyer's Method", note the following:

1) Jay uses language the Buddhist immediately understands. Jay takes the "Four Noble Truths" and makes them the "Four Noble Truths of Christ".

2) He is brief. This is not a complicated approach. However, he does not shy away from offering his friend the chance to start knowing Christ today.

3) This is an opening conversation. If, after this presentation, your friend does not accept Christ, do not be discouraged. This conversation hopefully will spark interest for your friend to have follow-up visits to discuss the two faiths.

4) As with all conversations, you can adapt it as you see fit. Read over the model conversation several times. Become familiar with the approach.

5) A key to understanding Buddhist barriers to the gospel is the biblical concept of heaven. Buddha directed his followers to go to a place of no more sin and suffering. When you describe heaven, emphasize that Jesus is from a Perfect Place of no sin, suffering, or death. Jay emphasized that stressing this idea of heaven is pivotal.

116

The "Lawyer's Method"

You: Hello my friend. How are you?

Friend: I am fine today.

You: Is your family well?

Friend: Yes, and yours?

You: They are fine. Would you mind if we talked for a moment?

Friend: Sure.

You: I know that you are a Buddhist and I am a Christian. I want to ask you about a difference in our religions.

Friend: That would be fine.

You: How do you reach Nirvana?

Friend: You must follow the Four Noble Truths and the Eightfold Path.

You: What do you mean?

Friend: The Four Noble Truths are:

1) Death is eminent.

2) Death and suffering is caused by sin.

3) One can eliminate suffering if one eliminates sin desire.

4) Desire and suffering is eliminated by living by the perfect standard.

You: What if you do not totally follow the Eightfold Path? Will that keep you from moving closer to Nirvana?

Friend: I'm not sure.

You: As far as I understand from what I've studied, Buddha demanded 100-percent perfection through meditation and good works. To move closer to Nirvana you cannot fail in those areas. If you fail, you will not advance to finally reach that level of deliverance.

Friend: We are commanded to try to live out the laws of Buddha.

You: You have your Four Noble Truths; may I share with you the Four Noble Truths of Christ?

Friend: Yes.

You: The Four Noble Truths of Christ are:

1) Suffering and death have an origin (a cause). Suffering and death is the effect of that cause.

2) The origin of death is sin. (Give a brief summary of Adam and Eve and their disobedience.)

3) A place without any further suffering and sin exists (heaven).

4) The Way out of the cycle of sin and suffering is faith in Christ's death, burial, and resurrection. Through His disciples Christ walks the Perfect Road. He makes them perfect in His eyes.

If a Buddhist commits one sin during his or her billions and billions of lives before attaining Nirvana, then the person will fall back down the ladder of reincarnation. Attaining a life in a higher abode (level) actually is a place in which sin is more likely and keeping Buddhist rules is much more difficult. Christ teaches His followers to repent and to believe the Good News. When we do this, His Holy Spirit enters our lives, adopts us, and makes us children of God and members of Christ's monkhood. He also calls His disciples to be baptized.

Jesus also demanded perfection but congratulated His disciples when they recognized that they cannot make themselves 100-percent perfect. Christ joyfully replied, *"With man this* (perfection) *is impossible, but with God all things are possible"* (Mt. 19:26). On the cross Christ made the way possible, but His victory over death did not end with death on the cross but with the resurrection.

Christ wants to give you victory over death and sin as well. He knows your life will have suffering now, but He provides a way for you to stand up under sin (1 Cor. 10:13) and to have ultimate victory over the problems of this world.

I gave my life to Christ (insert your date of conversion here) years ago. I still fail. I still mess up, but I know the God of the universe understands my sin and daily is helping me to improve. Plus, I know that after I die, GOD will be the One that saves me from the cycle of sin and suffering. I will not be saved by a set of rules that I know I cannot follow.

Would you consider the reality of Christ in your life as well?

(Option 2)

One can witness to Buddhists in other ways as well. Ricky Gordon, an independent missionary to Japan for more than 20 years, has extensive experience in church planting and evangelism among Buddhists. In his evangelism approach Gordon has a very conversational, relaxed style.[9] As you read two sample conversations that Gordon uses to open the conversation to talk about Christ, note several things.

1) First, Gordon gives two options. The first option enables you to talk about your friend's love for family as a bridge to the gospel. Your friend naturally will have an affection for a spouse, husband, father, mother, or child. From where does that affection spring? In Buddhist thought, your friend should be able to deny these natural affections. However, in our hearts we all know that loving our family members is right. Gordon gives us an extended conversation that shows that our love for our family is a sign of the reality of God.

2) Remember, these conversations are exact replications of discussions based in Japan. In whatever culture you live you will have to make some slight adaptations.

3) Gordon takes the reader through a discussion about death and the afterlife. Some degree of hope in the afterlife must exist. This second conversation is almost an

exact conversation that Gordon had just before this book was published. Because of the genuineness of the conversation this option has been included as a specific example.

4) The first page of conversation #1 simply is an example of an introductory conversation. Gordon is showing how the first few minutes must be centered on showing interest in the person. I have placed in bold the point at which Gordon moves from social conversation to the gospel witness and the dialogue that follows. Gordon did not take these conversations to the conclusion of the gospel. He is giving you an example of an introduction and how to explain who Christ is. He is assuming that you will have follow-up conversations. How to have the follow-up conversations is explained at the end of this section.

Conversation #1

You: Ken, It's good to see you again. Where have you been?

Friend: We've been so busy at work. With the economy slowing down, we haven't been able to hire any new people or replace the ones who retired.

You: So, your company is just dividing the load among those of you lucky enough to still have a job.

Friend: Right. But today's a national holiday, so I get some time off.

You: I love holidays here. This is about the only time I see complete families together. Usually when I visit the park, I'm the only father here. I see lots of young mothers with their kids; then, there's me.

Friend: That's true. Every chance I get, I try to spend with my family.

You: I'm always impressed with how much people here love children. You seem to really love your wife and children.

Friend: My working so much wouldn't have a lot of meaning if I had to come home to an empty apartment every night.

You: Were your father and mother like you? I mean, did you see this loving behavior modeled in your own home?

Friend: Not really. My dad worked all the time. When he was home, he usually was so tired, he slept a lot. But, when he could, especially on holidays like today, he'd take us to the park to play soccer or baseball. I do have fond memories of those times.

You: That's good.

Friend: I don't think anyone ever taught me to "love your family." I just instinctively knew that was a good thing.

You: I think that's true. It's like we're hardwired in our DNA to love our parents and siblings and then later our mates and children.

Friend: I think since our families are typically so small now, we especially lavish the love on our 1.29 children.

You: And they do grow up so fast.

Friend: Too fast.

You: I really enjoy watching all the interaction between the parents and children. Obviously they love each other. In some ways that's puzzling to me.

Friend: What do you mean?

You: On the first day of class I have my students introduce themselves. Then I ask them questions. Probably 95 percent of them identify themselves as Buddhist.

Friend: This is a Buddhist culture, so much of what we learn in school is based on Buddhist ideas.

You: Yes; you grew up in this culture. In school you were taught Buddhism.

Friend: Also, my first week at university we had to spend two days in a temple meditating and preparing ourselves for university life. So, what are you puzzled about?

You: What I see here in the park and what I know to be

true in your life seem to contradict one of the most important teachings in Buddhism.

Friend: Really? What's that?

You: Buddha taught that life is filled with suffering. Our suffering is from our attachment to the things of this life. To free ourselves from suffering and to end the cycle of reincarnation we must free ourselves from all natural feelings and desires. To reach Nirvana we must be free from all these worldly emotions.

Friend: I do remember being taught that at some point.

You: You remember being taught that, yet no one taught you to love. You just knew; you just believed that loving your parents, your wife, and your own flesh and blood was right and good.

Friend: I do enjoy my wife and children.

You: I read that just before his wife gave birth to their first son, Buddha left the home to meditate so that he would not experience great emotion and thus derive pleasure from the moment.

Friend: My wife would have killed me if I had walked out at that point!

You: Mine, too. I actually was in the delivery room for the births of all our children.

Friend: I didn't go that far, but I was there to give support until they took her away.

You: You and your wife know, instinctively, that loving and supporting each other is good and right.

Friend: I may not be such a good Buddhist. I don't really want to be free from my love for my family. Sometimes that's the only thing that keeps me going.

You: I know what you mean. This is a big difference between the Christian view and the Buddhist view. Moses wrote the first book of the Bible—Genesis. In it he tells that after

God created Adam and all the animals, God looked at Adam and said, "It's not good for the man to be alone." So he created a helper for him—the first woman. Family was God's idea.

Friend: So you're saying that what I know in my heart is more in line with Christianity than it is with Buddhism.

You: Yes, I think so. In the creation story Moses tells us that God made people in His own image and that the first human being became alive when God breathed His breath into Adam. King Solomon, considered to be the wisest man that ever lived, wrote that God has *planted eternity in men's hearts and minds* (Eccl. 3:10-11).

Friend: OK, you overwhelmed me a little bit. Rephrase that for a non-native English speaker, please.

You: Sorry. What I'm saying is that the love you feel for your wife and children was planted in your heart by God. We are made like God. One of Jesus' closest friends, John, explained that *God is love* (1 John 4:8). God's character is to love. So, your instinctive love for those closest to you was planted into your very DNA and that seed originated from God Himself.

Friend: Wow! I never thought of God in personal terms. I didn't know God actually had feelings.

You: Yes, He does. He has feelings. You have feelings. Your feelings for your family are natural and good.

Friend: As I watch my children grow and change, my feelings seem to grow, too. My attachment is getting stronger, not weaker.

You: Because you love them, you're willing to work long hours to give them what they want and need.

Friend: Whenever possible I try to give them the best.

You: God loves us so much, He gave His best. Jesus was trying to explain to a very high-level leader the nature of God.

He told the man, "God loved the world so much, He gave his only son." Then He said that anyone who believes in Him will not die but have eternal life. The best God had to give was His Son.

Friend: Who was He talking about? Who is God's Son?

You: Jesus was talking about Himself . . ..

Conversation #2

You: Liz, I haven't seen you since Fran's funeral. How long had the two of you been friends?

Friend: We had known each other for more than 30 years. How long had you known her?

You: We first met at a friend's house about 20 years ago. She visited our Bible study to learn English.

Friend: She went to your church, didn't she?

You: Yes, she did. We got to know each other pretty well over the years.

Friend: We worked at the same company for at least 15 years. We always talked about taking a trip to Europe together when we retired. Now that's impossible.

You: You can't take a trip together, but you can see her again.

Friend: What do you mean?

You: Fran was a Christian. Her body's gone, but our friend is in heaven. If you believe in Jesus, you can go to heaven, too.

Friend: But I love Buddha. I've been a Buddhist my whole life.

You: Fran was a Buddhist until she learned about Jesus.

Friend: So you believe the Fran we knew and loved is in heaven? I wish I could believe that.

You: When I first arrived here, I was teaching English to an elderly doctor. He actually spoke very good English. He was just trying to keep up his vocabulary by talking with me each week. One day we had a very interesting conversation.

Friend: About what?

You: He had basically retired. His son had taken over most of his practice. He was just taking care of his elderly patients. He said that when the last one died, he would be retired.

Friend: That sounds rather gloomy.

You: He told me he learned a lot from his patients as they were facing death.

Friend: Most of us don't want to think about dying, especially when we are young. What was your interesting conversation about?

You: When I arrived at his house one day, the first thing he said to me was, "You Christians have it easy when you die!" I had no idea what he was talking about, so I asked him to explain.

Friend: What did he mean?

You: He told me most of his patients were Buddhists, but a few were Christians. He said, "When we Buddhists face death, we are terrified! We have no idea what's going to happen to us. You Christians have it easy, because you know exactly where you are going and what it will be like."

Friend: Did he explain anything else?

You: He said his Christian patients passed away peacefully.

Friend: I heard that Fran died quietly in her sleep. I guess she had that kind of peace.

You: God wants everyone to have that kind of peace. We never know what's going to happen tomorrow. We all hoped Fran would get well and live a lot longer, but she didn't.

Friend: But what about Buddha?

You: Buddha wanted to show people the way to God, but he died. Jesus died but rose again. He told his followers, "Because I live, you will live also." Jesus had the victory over death, so He can show us the way, too.

Friend: That's a lot for me to believe.

You: Don't just believe me. You knew Fran when she was a

Buddhist and you knew her when she was a Christian. Did you see any change in her life?

Friend: Well, yes. She became a different person.

You: Based on watching her life for more than 30 years, you can decide: was she better with Buddha or better with Jesus?

Editor's note: After you have broached the subject of Jesus in either of these approaches, at this moment you can begin to tell your friend about what Christ has done in your life. You can give your personal testimony or take the friend through a simple plan of salvation.

If you choose your testimony, remember to make it brief. It can contain three basic sections.

1) Tell your friend about how your life was before you knew Christ. Describe your problems, struggles, etc.

2) Tell your friend how you gave your life to Christ. Explain that you had to surrender your life to Him.

3) Tell your friend the life change you've experienced. Describe your life with Christ.

If you choose to share the complete plan of salvation, you can use the Roman Road—Romans 3:23, 6:23, 5:8, 10:9, and finally 10:13. Walk the person through explaining the gospel. (For a more-detailed explanation of how to use these verses see the chapters on Catholicism and Protestantism.)

Questions a Buddhist Might Ask
or that You Might Ask a Buddhist

Unlike adherents of other religions a Buddhist might be less likely to question your belief system. In fact, since tolerance is a key component in the Buddhist's belief system, then logically the person won't try to question your faith. However, included are a few issues that could emerge.

1) Why can't I be a Buddhist and a Christian at the same time?

Your response: Jesus said, "*I am the way, the truth and the life. No one comes to the Father except through me*" (John 14:6).

To follow Christ requires a total commitment to Him as a person. One cannot be a follower of Christ and of another form of salvation at the same time. Christ is the One who sets the standards of how He is to be followed. We are not the ones who set them.

2) Can you not believe in reincarnation? A cycle of life certainly seems apparent. Just look at the seasons of the year and the cycle of life and death; I believe a cycle of reincarnation must exist.

Your response: Christians do not believe in reincarnation but instead believe in resurrection. We believe that if you have given your life to Christ, on your death your spirit will be with God. If you have rejected His Son, your spirit will be separated from Him. We believe that when He returns to judge us all, God will give us glorified bodies. The Bible teaches that we have one chance at this life; then we will face judgment (Heb. 9:27). However, for those who have given their lives to Christ, judgment is not something to dread but something to anticipate.

3) I think the idea of following only Jesus Christ is intolerant.

Your response: Something being intolerant is different from something being TRUE. Christ did not teach intolerance. He taught us to love our neighbors and to treat each other with respect. However, He also told us that the foundation for this love and respect occurs through Him. He is the basis of all Truth.

4) You say that Christ was here to free all people, but the world still has so much sadness in it.

Your response: Christ always spoke plainly to His followers about the realities of this world. He let us know that this world is broken with the reality of sin. The evil we do is real and damages our lives.

Evil and suffering are not in our imaginations; instead, they are very real. At some point you and I both have experienced true pain in this world. If you haven't yet, you will. No matter how much we meditate or try to do good deeds, this doesn't take away from the fact that we have true pain. Christ promises to give us an abundant life (John 10:10) and also to give us true relief from pain when we get to experience God for all eternity.

5) I do not believe we all are evil; we are born good.

Your response: Are you a parent? Do you teach a child to lie or be rebellious? Children inherently know how to do WRONG and must be taught how to do RIGHT. How do they know to do wrong? They know because they have been born with a sin nature. God allows us to be born into sin because He wants us to have two glorious gifts. The first of these gifts is freedom. This is the freedom to choose or not to choose to love Him. God does not force anyone to love Him. He wants our unconditional love and commitment. That occurs only as He gives us the freedom to choose to commit to Him. The second gift He wants us to have is the gift of grace. Only when we realize how far short we are to His perfection can we truly appreciate what a GIFT knowing Him is. We know Him in our sin because He first loved us.

God bless you as you attempt to share with your Buddhist friends.

---

[1]For a more thorough overview of the caste system see the chapter on Hinduism.

[2]Buddhists have done a phenomenal job of working cross-culturally. When one considers the wide variety of Asian, and now Western, countries that the religion has touched, Buddhism merits a great deal of respect missiologically. China, India, Afghanistan (in the early years of Buddhism), Laos, Vietnam, Cambodia, Japan, North and South Korea, Burma, and areas of Indonesia, to name only a few, are countries to which Buddhism quickly spread.

[3]Remember the TV show "Lost" on ABC? Remember the mysterious group of "others" called the Dharma Initiative? (If you didn't see "Lost" and don't know this obscure reference, please forgive me.) The point still stands that often we don't even realize through words how much these religions have infiltrated all aspects of our lives.

[4]*http://www.pbs.org/edens/thailand/buddhism.htm*

[5]Quote taken from Dr. Stan May, missions professor at Mid-America Baptist Theological Seminary, class lecture, 2006.

[6]Special thanks to Dr. Stan May's introductory notes on Buddhism. They served as a guide for the background section.

[7]The fact holds true for Muslims, Mormons, Animists, Hindus, Protestants, and Catholics as well. We are overly intimidated about talking about our faith because we assume people know about and reflect on their religion more than they actually do.

[8]Interview with Jay, December 2011. Because of security reasons Jay's full name has been withheld.

[9]Gordon, Ricky. Email interview, January 2012.

Chapter 8

How to Witness
to Your Hindu Friends

Witnessing to Hindus can be a daunting task. During a chapel service at our seminary a student went to the microphone and described how he witnessed to a Hindu. This young man had witnessed to a variety of individuals before, but when he was confronted with the possibility of witnessing to a Hindu, he said, "They have all of those gods. I just felt . . . helpless."

The world's Hindu population is around 960,000,000.[1] To understand how to interact with Hindus, accept the fact that the foundational beliefs of the religion present formidable arguments against Christianity. After all, with 330,000,000 gods, Hindus' simple response can be, "How can we be wrong, if we accept that everyone is at least partially right?"

Yet, at the same time Hindus around the world are trusting Christ. In India, a modern-day revival is occurring. India's Christian church has grown and is getting larger. According to Operation World it now comprises more than 70-million members. That makes it the eighth-largest Christian population in the world, just behind that of the Philippines and Nigeria, bigger than that of Germany and Ethiopia, and twice the size of the number of Christians in the United Kingdom.[2]

Global Religion?

Is Hinduism a global religion? Adherents numbering 960 million certainly point to that fact. However, if one considers that

901 million are found in one nation alone—India—then the global reach of the religion seems much less prominent.[3] However, an estimated 1,334,000 Hindus are in the United States alone. The ideology of Hinduism has impacted the way of thinking of tens of millions of people in the West.

The universal and relativistic mindset of Hinduism has made its mark. "Hinduism is the most accommodating of all religions. In a world full of strife, the 'accommodative' spirit and the planks of universalism and relativism, as well as the other cultivated characteristics of modern Hinduism, become very attractive to so many diverse groups of people that the Hindus have truly come to see their faith as a relevant global religion."[4]

Who Is a Hindu? How Would You Describe the Beliefs of a Hindu Today?

Unlike Islam and Christianity, with a definite core set of beliefs, Hinduism is far more difficult to define. In fact, even the name *Hinduism* is not entirely accurate. The term *Hinduism* was created by Western scholars in an attempt to organize the multitude of religions in India under one banner. Hindus will have a different set of beliefs and practices depending on their geographic region in India. If they are not from India, their set of beliefs will vary depending on their teachers. Consequently, pinpointing a Hindu's beliefs exactly is difficult. To a Westerner this may seem contradictory, but in fact, in Hinduism contradiction does not mean error.

How then can we understand this belief system? In his work, *Sharing Your Faith With a Hindu*, Madasamy Thirumalai gives eight summary statements about Hindus; these statements should help clear up the fog of the religion itself.[5] The eight statements that you will read are from Thirumalai's work; for clarification I will add thoughts to the eight.

• **Hindus primarily are from India.**

This fact already has been highlighted. Numerically speaking Hinduism is an Indian religion. However, this point brings about a great truth. To Hindus the land of India itself is considered holy. If you are witnessing to a Hindu, most Hindus will feel a certain defensiveness about their faith in terms of NATIONALISM. To be Indian is to be Hindu.[6] These two identities are inexorably linked.

• **Hindus worship idols, images, pictures, relics, and other objects.**

Some Hindus find salvation through knowledge and some through asceticism, but many Hindus find salvation through revering idols. To us, some of the idols and images can look quite gruesome. You might see snakes and elephant heads and a variety of beasts interwoven into one supposed deity represented in the idol. For the typical Westerner, images of these deities at best seem scary and at worst seem nonsensical. However, these incongruent images have a purpose. In realistic terms you can't have a woman with four arms who is blueish in color (the goddess Lakshmi, wife of Vishnu, who also is pictured in blue); you also can't have a person with multiple heads (the god Brahma). Since these types of physical attributes can't happen in our world, the images are supposed to guide the viewer to understanding how unknowable and transcendent these deities are from us.

• **Hindus believe in rebirth and *karma*.**

Reincarnation is a key element in Hindu philosophy. The fact that every action of life has a consequence for good or for bad is known as *karma*. You are on a continual cycle of birth and rebirth. Your works-based life of *karma* will help you get off this cycle. The term for leaving this perpetual cycle is *moksha*.

• **Hindus are pantheistic, polytheistic (actually henotheistic), and animistic practitioners of religion.**

Hindus can be pantheistic, which means they believe that

everything is god. They also believe in a polytheistic world. After all, if you can accept that the reality of 330,000,000 gods, that's VERY polytheistic. However, their polytheism has a twist. Depending on who you ask, they can believe in *polytheism* (multiple gods) or *monotheism* (one god—Brahmin). They actually believe that you can have both "isms" at the same time. The one Supreme God can appear to different individuals as different gods (*henotheism*). Consequently, you cannot define Hinduism as simply polytheistic or monotheistic.

Finally, Hindus are animistic. If you have read the chapter on animism, this should not surprise you. Just as animism has affected Christianity and Islam, it also has influenced Hinduism.

• Hindus usually are governed by the social system of caste.

Although officially illegal to discriminate on the basis of caste in India today, this particular social order still plays a major role in Hindu thought. (NEVER, EVER ask people what caste they are from. This is highly offensive). Your caste determines everything from your profession and marriage to social etiquette.

Hinduism contains four levels of caste. These terms can be complicated to remember. As a word of warning under these larger categories Hinduism has many subsets. However, a Hindu's lot in life drastically changes depending on whether you are part of the:

• *Brahmins* (Priests)
• *Kshatriya* (Warriors)
• *Vaishyas* (Business/Produce)
• *Shudras* (Servants)

The first three castes are called "twice-born". They have made progression on the road to *moksha* (liberation). The final sections of people below these castes are called the *untouchables*. This class of people does not form a caste. The untouchables are at the bottom of the social hierarchy. These castes also are known as *varanas*, which can mean "colors". Some scholars think the caste system may have been founded as sort of an implied racism. In terms of percentage the highest castes tend to be more light-skinned in color; this lends some credence to this idea.[7]

As a Christian be aware of two aspects of the caste system. First, a Hindu will deny the fact that the caste system involves systemic racism. The caste system simply is one's lot in life in terms of birth. For these people color is not a factor. Secondly, to offer help to someone from a lower caste actually hinders that person's path to liberation.

This second point is pivotal. Ultimately, if people surrender their lives to Christ, this can be viewed as an aberrant elevation of their lot in life. From the Hindu perspective, people must fulfill their duty in this life in whatever situation they are in. If they don't fulfill their duty as lower-caste members, they cannot progress. Any decision that improves one's lot in life will be vehemently fought against by friends and neighbors. Families will think they are protecting the person from making a decision that will undermine his progress to *moksha*. This is a serious difference in the value of the individual according to the Bible. Christ elevates a person to being equal to all people (Gal. 3:28). This core truth is the antithesis of the caste system.

• **Hindus are known for their tolerance and acceptance of a wide variety of theological beliefs within their religion.**

To add Christ to their pantheon of gods is not very problematic for a Hindu. After all, if one believes in the possibility of millions of gods, then adding one more won't be very difficult. For example, to a Hindu, if Brahmin (the supreme God, not the caste) can manifest as a variety of gods, why can't he manifest as Jesus Christ?

• **Continuity, not change, dominates the concerns of Hindus.**

In the United States the highest virtues in our national

heritage are freedom, honesty, or independence. For a Hindu the highest virtue is duty. Fulfilling one's obligations to family and community is more important than are individualism virtues we might prioritize in the West. Therefore, staying within your caste and believing as your parents did is critical for Hindus.

• **As in other religions, a vast gulf exists between the elitist and folk religious forms and practices of Hinduism.**

Unfortunately, the word *folk* often causes one to equate that idea with "hick" or "ignorant." Do not make that mistake with a folk Hindu—one who places great emphasis on the worship of idols and rituals. With more than 1,000,000,000 people, India and Nepal have no shortage of extremely intelligent "folk" Hindus.

Practitioners of Hinduism vary greatly in their religious values. Some think that an intellectual study of the Scriptures (called the *Vedas*) will help them attain *moksha*. Others believe that ritualistic practices to idols will give them liberation. Ultimately a certain amount of dialogue must occur to fully understand the Hindu's preferred path to salvation.

Common Questions about Hinduism[8]

What scriptures do they study? (Get ready for a LOT of big words in this paragraph).

Only the Hindus that are approaching liberation through the "way of knowledge" (see below) are likely to study their scriptures. Hindus have two classes of scriptures: *shruti* and *smitri*. *Shruti* ("heard") are considered inspired, and were heard by seers ages ago. They include four *Vedas*: *Rig Veda, Yajur Veda, Sama Veda* and *Atharva Veda*. Each *Veda* has a series of supplementary books called the *Brahmanas* and *Sutras* (each having a different name). Also included are the *Upanishads,* which are the appendix to the *Vedas*. Typically only the priests know the *Vedas*; however, some Hindus will have read the *Upanishads*. The *Smitri* ("handed down") do not have the same level of inspiration, but Hindus are more likely to know about them. They have the two main epics, the Mahabharata and Puranas (narratives of the gods). Within the Mahabharata is the Bhagavad Gita, which is a conversation between Krishna and the hero named Arjuna. Krishna teaches Arjuna to follow him as well as teaches the importance of keeping caste duties. The Bhagavad Gita is the scripture of which Hindus are most likely to be aware.

Do I need to remember any of the 330 million gods?

Each individual geographic region has specific gods on which they focus. Be aware of at least three supreme deities.

1. Brahman—the creator god. While Hindus have no school of devotion specific to him, in many temples he is a regular fixture.

2. Shiva—the destroyer god and the god of reproduction. Shiva's wife is Parvati. Sometimes he is depicting as having affairs with Kali. The city of Calcutta was named after Kali.

3. Vishnu—He is the preserver god of the *dharma* (the way of the gods.)[9] Many times throughout history Vishnu has returned in human or animal form. In the 10th manifestation of Vishnu, he will return as Kalki on a white horse. Practitioners of Hare Krishna worship Krishna, who is the eighth manifestation of Vishnu.

These are the three principal gods of Hindus. Christians immediately see a parallel between this Trinitarian view of their high gods and our own view of the Trinity. However, avoid stressing this parallel. After all, Brahma can appear as many gods, so the view of their trinity is more henotheistic than it is monotheistic.

On the practical side several other gods that Hindus are likely to revere are Ganesha, the elephant-headed remover of obstacles, and Krishna, technically an avatar of Vishnu but often worshiped as a god. Finally, among the common people is Lakshmi (for good fortune and wealth) and Sarasvati, the goddess of learning important to students and teachers.

How important is yoga?

The idea of yoga has become a touchy subject. In one sense many Christians aren't sure whether they should practice yoga. On the other hand, since one-third of the people that I know have tried the P90X® extreme workout program (notice I didn't say one-third of my friends COMPLETED P90X®), they've all tried their hand at yoga. Many Hindus complain that Christians have taken their spiritual practice and turned it into a simple exercise.

Christians need to understand that the purpose of yoga IS linked with Hindu belief. It centers on the concept that we can clear our minds to try to join Brahman through meditation. Christians should be aware that yoga, at its core, is not something with which one should trifle. Its purpose, by design, is to become one with a deity.

Can't Christians use yoga for prayer? For yoga the goal is to empty one's mind. For Christians the purpose of meditation and prayer is to fill one's mind with Scripture and hear from God. Of all the issues to be discussing with your Hindu friend, stressing this area of his belief initially is not important. However, do not be fooled into believing that yoga ultimately is harmless and has no spiritual aspect.

In Hinduism how is one saved?

Hinduism promulgates three means to salvation:

1) *Karma marga*—the way of works—performing caste duties, rituals

2) *Gnana marga*—the way of knowledge—using the intellect, studying Upanishads. In this form some believe that a person is comprised of the Atman, which is identical to Brahman (the impersonal god who is all around us.) Through discipline and

mediation one can arrive at the realization of his or her Atman. Most Hindus will not be aware of this practice, however; only those who are of the intellectual elite will do so.

3) *Bhakti marga*—way of love and devotion to gods. Worship and praise take precedence over rituals.[10]

In a nutshell what would you say about Hindus and their beliefs?

Ultimately, if you encounter Hindus from South Asia, they more than likely will believe the following:

He or she no doubt would believe in *karma* and *samsara*, revere certain texts and certain deities (usually without naming a single text or deity as requisite), accept the obligation of satisfying his or her older ancestors and caste status within a social structure that most Hindus would recognize, demonstrate certain ascetic tendencies in the form of fasts and vows, and describe certain progress or intentions in living goals and pursuits toward an ultimate release (although for many the ideal of *moksha* is a remote target at the far end of an inevitable series of rebirths.)[11]

To put that quote into simpler English, a Hindu probably will believe:

1) The person's actions–*karma*—have consequences.

2) Life has an endless cycle of rebirths—*samsara*.

3) Duty in life is of the utmost importance; Hindus must accept their stations in life—caste.

4) A certain amount of asceticism, or self-denial, is a good thing for a Hindu.

5) A system of reward for actions is done here. Most will not think about their ultimate release from their cycle of rebirths

because it seemingly is so far off.

How to Share Your Faith with Your Hindu Friends

How do you use this knowledge as a bridge to the gospel in sharing your faith? As with all the other chapters, four universal steps begin the process of sharing your faith with Hindus. They are:

1) Befriend them.
2) Avoid the urge to **just** be their friend and never engage in a spiritual conversation.
3) Look for the spiritual clues.
4) Seize the initiative even if spiritual clues do not present themselves.

For a detailed look at these four ideas, please refer to pages 33-37. Once you have taken a few moments to review these four steps, then you are ready to examine different approaches to talk with your Hindu friend. Let us examine a few of these approaches.

The first set of approaches are from Anjan.[12] Anjan is an Indian church planter who in the last five years has seen several thousand Hindus trust Christ as Savior. Did he lead all these nationals to Christ by himself? No, he taught fundamental principles of evangelism to a circle of men who then went out and trained others in evangelism (2 Tim. 2:2). He is an extremely competent evangelist who has agreed to help in the completion of this book. Anjan shared two recent, actual conversations that he has had with Hindus. These are actual conversations that he used to share the gospel.

Note two things about Anjan's approach:

1) **His approach is simple**. Anjan is an Indian believer who shares how he bridged the gospel to his Hindu friends. This first conversation consists of nothing overly profound but is extremely practical. He asks an introductory question, points out that we are sinners, and gives a solution. This approach is not much different from that of the Roman Road.

2) **Anjan does not give a gospel appeal.** At the end you might NEED to give a gospel appeal. See pages 37-42 to see how to lead someone in a gospel appeal for salvation.

A Conversation between a Christian and Hindu

Christian: May I ask you some spiritual questions?

Hindu: Yes.

Christian: How can I get to heaven?

Hindu: If you do your duties and do good to others and live a holy life, you will do well.

Christian: After doing all these good things, how do I know for sure? I want to do good, but many times I do what I do not want.

Hindu: I just do not how one can be sure. This is what our religion says. Through *karma* (works) one can be redeemed from Samsara (world).

Christian: But our religion says, *No one is righteous but all have sinned and come short of glory of God* (Rom. 3) Therefore I inherit sin from my forefathers. But we have the Good News that, *"For God so loved the world that He gave His only begotten Son, that whoever believes in Him should not perish but have everlasting life"* (John 3:16).

Hindu: How?

Christian: A long time ago God promised He would send a Messiah—the Holy and Righteous One. God showed how He would send Him, where He would send Him, and for what

140

purpose. God gave us all the details. In the fullness of time God did send the Messiah and offered Himself as the only Holy and Acceptable Sacrifice on the cross of Calvary to God for all humanity once for all. Also, He rose from death and still is alive.

Hindu: How do I know that He has borne my sins?

Christian: The Bible says, *We all have wandered away like sheep have gone astray, but the Lord has put on Him the punishment for all* (including yours) *the evil we* (including you) *have done* (author's paraphrase of Isa. 53:6). Therefore, Jesus Christ owns the salvation for all humanity.

Hindu: If it is so, what do I have to do now?

Christian: First, try to recollect the sins you have committed. Then you confess to God and repent for those sins. Ask God to forgive you. Invite Jesus into your heart and say that you will follow him day by day.

Hindu: Yes, I feel much relieved now; I thank God and you for helping me.

(Anjan's second approach)
Note two things about this approach:

1) Anjan described this as a follow-up visit. During the research for this book he stressed that among Hindus gospel tracts are very productive. You might need to consider buying some simple gospel tracts to give to your friends.

2) Again note Anjan's simple approach. Often we try to overcomplicate the message. Instead, as quickly as possible Anjan takes the person to the gospel.

3) Remember, this is an actual conversation that occurred right before the book went to the publisher.

Hindu: I am very happy to read the tract you gave me last time. I found something very positive about life and the love of God for me.

Christian: Thank you! Many people buy a "life insurance" policy to ensure their family's lives after their death, but they lose their own lives since their lives are not eternally secured. The Bible says that one can gain the whole world but lose his or her own soul (Mark 8:36).

Hindu: You are very true. Please share more about this truth.

Christian: I mean the lives we live on this earth will end here. After this life is an eternal life. If we are redeemed, then we shall live in heaven eternally; if we are not redeemed, we are condemned eternally in hell. Our today decides tomorrow.

Hindu: How can I trust the Bible? Our religion is much older than Christianity is.

Christian: One of the strongest proofs of the authenticity of the Bible is that whatever the Bible prophesied a long time ago already has been fulfilled. Some prophecies are yet to be fulfilled, since we see things conforming to the present world. The Bible is full of prophesies, since only God knows the future; hence the Bible is God's Word. Secondly, Christianity has its root in the Old Testament, which starts with the beginning of the universe.

Hindu: OK, I agree. But why so much corruption in the Christian countries? Why is the Christian society so weak with families that are broken?

Christian: Christianity is not a religion one can possess by physical birth; a person does so by personal choice. Therefore, a person born in a Christian family does not necessarily become a Christian. Similarly those who attend the church do not necessarily become Christians.

Also the Christian faith is not a matter of a one-day experience; it is a lifelong experience. A person who day by day grows spiritually becomes a strong follower of Jesus. If people don't grow in Christ, their lives do not conform to the Bible and to the life of Jesus. Hence, we can see plenty of good and bad examples of Christians.

Hindu: Let us meet again.

Christian: I want to pray for you and your family. Do you have any problem in your family that I can pray for?

Hindu: (He brought his mother) Please pray for my mother, who has been suffering from back pain for several years.

Christian: (Prayer was offered; his mother got immediate relief. The Christian went away for that day. The next time when the Christian returned, the following occurred).

Christian: Hello. How are you!

Hindu: Oh, it is a miracle! We had showed my mother to many doctors and even prayed to our gods many times, but nothing happened. But now she has no back pain since you visited last and Jesus has healed her. We want to accept Jesus, because He is the true God.

Editor's note—Remember: be a person of prayer. Anjan's second conversation is an exact re-creation of a dialogue he had several weeks before this book was completed. God can use the miraculous to reveal Himself at any time—including to your Hindu friend.

(Option 2)

I asked "David S."[13] , a veteran pastor who has served in India for more than 11 years, to describe his witnessing approach. Notice David's brief, nonintimidating style. David looks for a person's needs and then shows how Christ fulfills those needs. Also, note how many times David refers to the "One True God". He constantly points this polytheistic friend to God.

David said:

I always start a conversation with the topic of my friend's family, such as his mother, father, wife, or children. I then continue the conversation by inquiring about their needs. I keep the conversation going until I find some place that isn't going well in his life. For example, Indians value education. If their children are trying to get into college and a child is facing examination, that family is under stress. In truth, whatever their child is involved in that is difficult would be an area I'd stress. Other examples might involve:

1) People trying to conceive their first child or people trying to get a visa to visit (or to stay in) America.

2) Health issues are highly important. Indian communities actually are experiencing an epidemic of diabetes and heart disease.

Whatever the stress in his or her life, I would ask, "How are you feeling about it? Is it worrying you?"

At this point I let my friend respond.

Whatever his specific needs, I express my concern and say, "I believe in the One True God because He really loves me. I will pray for you. The One True God knows your problem and knows about you." Then I say, "Wow, I really am concerned. Would you mind if I pray with you right now?" I would bow my head and clasp my hands in a posture of prayer. If my friend is a man, I will put my hand on his shoulder and pray RIGHT THEN for that need.

With that prayer I have ministered to my friend immediately. I then again express concern by saying, "I know this is troublesome for you."

Then I think of a story in the Bible that would match his dilemma.

For example, if my friend and his wife cannot conceive, I pick the biblical story of Hannah to show God's concern for people trying to conceive (1 Sam. 1 and 2). If my friend is suffering from mental frustration, to show Christ's concern for the anguished I tell the story of the demoniac (Mark 5).

I then say to my friend, "Your situation is just like the story of . . . " and then tell that story.

If you are concerned about recalling the correct story, remind yourself that God will help you recall a story from Scripture. You don't have to tell every detail—just what you can remember. (If you already know your friend's issues, you might feel more comfortable if beforehand you research and familiarize yourself with different stories in Scripture that might parallel your friend's difficulties).

If the conversation still is going well, I tell my friend, "I had great favor from the One True God."

I then share my testimony. (I do this to attribute the blessing of the One True God to myself). I then tell my friend:

"But all those blessings did not make me a true believer. Those were a kindness to me from the One True God. The kindness stemmed from listening to a Bible story from a pastor. I decided that I needed salvation. I knew I needed to be forgiven for my sins. My father was very wise. My father, being the spiritual man that he was, encouraged me to give my life to Jesus; that made me a true believer. Now I have a personal salvation. I made my decision for Christ not just for my family but because I knew it was true." (*Editor's note: Your testimony obviously will be different from that of David's, but notice how David put his testimony in terms the Hindu could understand. He included his father and gave him due honor.*)

At this point I might give my friend an opportunity to give his life to Christ; however, I probably will wait to do so. Why? I wait, generally, because he still will have to deal with many issues such as idolatry and polytheism. You don't want to rush the process.

Here are several key things David stresses for our attention:
1) When you witness, don't go so fast that your friends

merely add Jesus to their pantheon of gods. Don't just throw everything at them at once. They've got a lot to process.

2) If you are dealing with devout, high-class Brahmans, they may say that your religion is Western but that it is not for them. Talk about the apostle Thomas in the first century. Say that Thomas almost immediately after Christ's earthly ministry went to India and established the church. The Indian church is as old as any church in the world.

3) If you get a little farther along in witnessing to your friend, you can address the One True God and the issue of idolatry. Eventually you might want to say, "Suppose you are walking down the street, see your father, and then move aside to address another man as 'father'. You do this while your actual father is watching. What if you even stoop down and touch the other man's feet (a sign of respect)? How would your father feel? In the same way we do this to God the Father when we give honor to lesser gods."

(Option 3)

Jayakar Danam, minister with His Sanctuary Ministries, which has planted 23 churches in India, agreed to share a typical conversation one might have with a Hindu. Jayakar studies in the United States. His approach does an excellent job of bridging the West to the East.

Note a few items about Jayakar's approach:

1) Jayakar, as well as Anjan, does not overcomplicate the message.

2) Jayakar actually states that being interested in a god is positive. Jayakar says, "It is better if the person believes in some god than no god at all." For Jayakar this mindset can give the Christian a common ground with the Hindu.

3) Jayakar's section in this book is not an exact conversation that he has had recently. Instead, this is a step-by-step guide for

the reader to copy as he or she witnesses.

Jayakar said:

You have to see Hindus as you would any other person with whom you would share your faith. Assess them. Look at their facial expressions. If you determine that the Hindu is open and friendly at the moment, you may ask, "What made you travel to America?"

Then take a moment to introduce yourself. I do not tell them I'm a Christian so early on, because at this stage that might be offensive. If you are uncomfortable talking about their religion from the onset, ask them some issues about Indian culture. They will be very open to tell about their heritage. Some things are very important in Indian culture. Dance is very important. Food is very important, because each state in India has its own specific foods. Hindus will be proud to discuss their food. This might lead the conversation to their religion, since it is such a part of the Indian heritage.

If not, over time you can switch to the topic of religion. You can say, "I have heard that Indians are very traditional in the area of religion and that their religion is very ancient. What are your religious beliefs?" You let them respond; typically they will be enthusiastic to respond. No matter from what caste a particular Hindu originates, the person will take pride in the fact that he or she is a Hindu.

Then ask, "What makes you believe in your particular god?"

This is VERY important. When the Hindu describes his or her particular god, you can learn what that Hindu is seeking to be fulfilled. Why? In Hinduism each individual god supposedly meets a particular need of a person. This is one of the reasons why the person worships that god. (At a later time in the witness we then will contrast this god with the one perfect God.)

You then may say, "I am glad you believe in something. I appreciate that you are (smart, sensitive, etc.) enough to believe in a god. Many people do not believe in a god in this world."

I then ask, "What is the attribute of your god that you like the most?" After the Hindu responds, ask, "What do you think a god should be like?" Typically the person will say that a god should be "holy or all-powerful". At this point say you appreciate what the person has said.

Ask, "Of all the gods that you see worshiped, do you see all the attributes that you would like in any of these gods?" This question will be difficult to hear, but truth can be painful. The Christian now is ready to show the difference between the Hindu god and the Eternal God.

Briefly I tell my friend that I believe in a perfect God in all His attributes. Because He is perfect, He can deal with our sin. I have to tell my friend what *sin* is. For a Hindu *sin* is to steal or kill. I explain that sin actually is an act against the Holy God.

I discuss that in life a person has constant frustration with trying to know Truth. If a perfect God really exists, we have trouble seeing Him. I explain how we are shrouded from the truth. I read Romans 3:23 to show that we all are sinners and we have failed.

I then give my testimony. Even though I was reared in a Christian home in India, I still was very sinful. However, the perfect God changed me. When I discuss with my friend what God did for me, this helps show that the perfect God is REAL to me.

At this point, I discuss Jeremiah 17:9, which tells us that our *heart is deceitful above all things*. I say a deficit in our hearts keep us from knowing the truth. Even sometimes as Christians we are deceived. For example a Hindu believes in reincarnation and that we can do things to make ourselves better in the next life. Sometimes Christians do the same things. We think we ourselves can do many things to PLEASE God and to make things better. In a sense we think by our work, we can better ourselves. In fact, the Bible says the opposite. We are to have faith in Him and let Him work through us to better us. In fact, without faith pleasing God is impossible (Heb. 11:6).

(We have just shown the parallel between reincarnation and believing we have to work to please God. We are trying to show the Hindu that we are sinners just like your friend is. We all can be deceived. I even might use Gal. 3:28 here.)

I tell my friend that because God is holy, in our sinful natures we cannot stand before Him. We are separated from God. Our minds are captivated by the things of human nature. Sin has separated us from the glory of God. I tell my friend that "glory" should not make us think of the brightness of a metal in an idol but in the actual holiness of God.

Even though we can't stand in God's presence, He still loves us. Just as a father loves his child even when that child has done wrong, God still loves us. He knows we will do wrong. God gave us the free will to choose to be holy like Him or to do wrong. However, we still can see a gap between God and us. Our sin has separated us from God (recall the definition of *sin*).

Then I quote John 3:16. I describe Who Christ is (born of a virgin in a nonsexual way, died on a cross, rose from the grave). I tell my friend that the resurrection has power for our lives. Many people think this resurrection is foolishness (1 Cor. 1:18). However, no god in any religion in the world today can claim to have died and returned; only Christ can claim that. Christ died and rose again so that we could be made right with God. When Christ died on the cross, He provided a bridge between God and humanity if we believe on Him. He took the punishment for sin on the cross. If we believe, we can be reconciled to God.

I then say, "I stand before you being reconciled to God because of my belief in Him. If you give your life to Him, He can change you inside" (Gal. 2:21). This doesn't mean you will avoid sin, but you will have salvation. When you die, you will resurrect from the grave and not reincarnate from the grave.

I can lead the friend in a prayer and say, "Today you can

choose life or death" (Deut. 30:19). Today, if you were to die, what is your hope? My hope is that I will live again and live with God. I have to share this gospel with you because of the joy within me.

Finally, I can give the invitation. I will ask whether the person wants the privilege of knowing the One True God. I might read Psalm 139, which says:

O LORD, You have searched me and known me.
You know my sitting down and my rising up;
You understand my thought afar off.
You comprehend my path and my lying down,
And are acquainted with all my ways.
For there is not a word on my tongue,
But behold, O LORD, You know it altogether.
You have hedged me behind and before,
And laid Your hand upon me.
Such knowledge is too wonderful for me;
It is high, I cannot attain it.
Where can I go from Your Spirit?
Or where can I flee from Your presence?
If I ascend into heaven, You are there;
If I make my bed in hell, behold, You are there.
If I take the wings of the morning,
And dwell in the uttermost parts of the sea,
Even there Your hand shall lead me,
And Your right hand shall hold me.
If I say, "Surely the darkness shall fall on me,"
Even the night shall be light about me;
Indeed, the darkness shall not hide from You,
But the night shines as the day;
The darkness and the light are both alike to You.
For You formed my inward parts;

You covered me in my mother's womb.
I will praise You, for I am fearfully and wonderfully made;
Marvelous are Your works,
And that my soul knows very well.
My frame was not hidden from You,
When I was made in secret,
And skillfully wrought in the lowest parts of the earth.
Your eyes saw my substance, being yet unformed.
And in Your book they all were written,
The days fashioned for me,
When as yet there were none of them.
How precious also are Your thoughts to me, O God!
How great is the sum of them!
If I should count them, they would be more in number
    than the sand;
When I awake, I am still with You.
Oh, that You would slay the wicked, O God!
Depart from me, therefore, you bloodthirsty men.
For they speak against You wickedly;
Your enemies take Your name in vain.
Do I not hate them, O LORD, who hate You?
And do I not loathe those who rise up against You?
I hate them with perfect hatred;
I count them my enemies.
Search me, O God, and know my heart;
Try me, and know my anxieties;
And see if there is any wicked way in me,
And lead me in the way everlasting.

Then I offer to lead the person in a sinner's prayer, or I present a tract or Bible. If the Hindu is not ready, I advise the person to pray that the One True God will reveal Himself. I believe God truly will.

Jayakar gave a few additional points. You may or may not choose to use them.

1) When you are discussing idols: Ask the Hindu, "If you have a child, do you want your child to be in the image of the idol you worship?" The idols often are very scary. God created us to be in His good image.

2) When discussing tradition: Somewhere in your fore-fathers' time, they have gone astray from the One True God. They began to worship other gods. Probably you follow your god because your parents did; you are se-cretly afraid. You have fear in your heart for idols. Don't let fear get in the way of your intellect.

3) When discussing idols: Does a potter, when molding a pot, allow the clay to dictate what to do? Yet that occurs in India. Someone makes the idols, but they become the god. Do you think the idol is more than wood and stone? Even in the marketplace in India they are called *idols*. They represent gods that are not all-powerful; let me tell you about the one powerful God.

4) Scripture tells us that no one has seen God at any time. Poets, authors and artists have done a good job try-ing to describe Him as powerful and that no one can imagine Him. Unfortunately people believe in images of the true God rather than the God Himself. The Bible says we should worship Him in Spirit and Truth (John 4:24).

(Option 4)

Dr. John Charping spent six years as a missionary in the country of Nepal. Through the years he and his family have min-istered to hundreds and hundreds of Hindus. Charping takes a "storying" approach to sharing his faith with Hindus.[14] As you re-view his approach, note the following:

1) Charping has given you a plan that you can read aloud in one setting or a seven-step guideline that you can follow to take the process more slowly.

2) Charping's approach centers on retelling the story of Scripture. Note: he bridges into the Christian message concepts that are critical to a Hindu.

3) The focus on this approach is *karma* (result of actions of this life) and *dharma* (one's role in this present life). Note how Charping points out the fruitlessness of trying to affect one's *karma* by dutifully fulfilling all of one's roles in life.

Charping said:

The following is one approach to sharing the gospel with a person from a Hindu background. The intent is to build a versatile framework that a person may use to effectively share the gospel.

Within Hinduism, Brahma is the creator god. Hindus believe that after creating the world, Brahma removed himself from any active role in the lives of humankind. At birth an impersonal fate imposes the previous life's *karma* on the present life, which in turn determines the present life's *dharma*. In Hinduism the blessings and cursings of this life are the result of *karma*. *Karma* is the effect of actions made in a previous life. *Dharma* is one's role in this present life; adherence or defiance to this role will result in merit in the next life. In other words, submission to the *dharma* of one life becomes the basis of the *karma* in the next.

On a global level Hinduism attempts to make peace with the universe through the stabilizing forces of *karma* and *dharma*. On a practical level Hindus are more likely to be concerned about struggles such as crop failure, infrequency of catching fish or game, sickness, infertility, and death. Their attention turns to appeasing local demons, spirits, and ancestors.

Hindus must understand that their present standing is not the result of their *karma* but results from the consequence of the fall of Adam and Eve. They must understand that their present actions—their *dharma*—will not afford them a better future but rather will solidify their own judgment. They must recognize that continual observance of rituals neither can atone for our actions nor address the root issue of our sin condition.

Sharing the gospel with a Hindu begins with establishing the character and activity of God. The conversation should include discussion on the sinfulness of humankind and the origin of humankind's fallen condition. The exchange should demonstrate the person and work of Christ Who not only is triumphant over those things that daily plague a person (i.e. demons, disease, death, and nature) but Who ultimately is triumphant over our main problem—sin.

Many preachers use three points to make the one point in their message. Many times these points can be developed further to create greater depth in the message. For the sake of simplicity and mnemonic value, our gospel presentation contains seven points that can be developed further as needed. The seven points of our gospel presentation include: The Creation, The Curse, The Conscience, The Calendar, The Cross, The Christ, and The Coming.[15]

The Creation
The Most High God of the universe has revealed Himself in the Bible. He begins by declaring Himself the Creator of all things (Gen. 1:1). In revealing His acts of creation, God created humankind unique from all forms of life. The first man and woman were called *Adam* and *Eve*. God created them in His image so that they might be in a relationship with Him and be in a position of honor and authority over all creation (Gen. 1:26).

The Curse

As Creator, the Most High God of the Bible requires His creation to be subject to Himself. Holiness is His most distinctive characteristic. God is wise and loving; His instruction to humankind is the highest wisdom. When He created Adam and Eve, He placed them in the Garden of Eden and allowed Adam to eat freely from any tree of the garden except from the tree of the knowledge of good and evil. He warned Adam that he would die if he ate from that tree (Gen. 2:17).

One day Satan spoke through a snake to tempt Eve to eat from the tree of the knowledge of good and evil. He deceived her and convinced her that eating from the tree would make her wise like God and not cause her death. Eve considered what Satan told her and decided to eat from the tree. Both Adam and Eve ate from the tree of the knowledge of good and evil.

In that moment Adam and Eve died spiritually. Their innocence was gone. They attempted to cover their shame and nakedness by making clothes from fig leaves. Afraid, they hid themselves from God. When God confronted Adam, he blamed Eve for the choice of eating from the tree of the knowledge of good and evil. When God questioned Eve, she blamed the snake for her choice (Gen. 3:1-13).

God did two things in reaction to Adam and Eve's disobedience. First, He promised that He would send a Deliverer to humankind. He prophesied that though Satan would attack the Deliverer, He ultimately would crush Satan's head (Gen. 3:15). Secondly, God cursed His created world and the bodies of humankind. God intended the curse to be a constant reminder of the broken relationship between God and humankind and of our need of God in every detail of life. The curse is a daily reminder that nothing in creation can function according to design without proper relationship to God (Rom. 8:20-23). The judgment of God on Adam and Eve—and not *karma*—is the reason for the pain and suffering in this present life.

The Conscience
Most Hindus do not have access to God's law given in the Bible. Nonetheless, God has made the conscience to function like the law (Rom. 2:13-14; Gal. 3:24). The message of the curse communicates the fact that something is wrong between the Creator and His creation, but the message of the conscience is more personal. The message of the conscience pricks the heart of a person to want to be and do what is right and honorable. The conscience has such power over a person that he or she is willing to go to great lengths either to appease or excuse the conscience.

In Hinduism, *sin* is better understood as the effects of *karma* and one's faithfulness or unfaithfulness to his *dharma*. Hindus do not understand the root condition of depravity. Hindus consider sin to be the result of an individual's actions and not the expression of a universal sin condition.

The seeking out of the services of a Hindu priest is a continual reminder that something is wrong in the conscience. Every sacrifice offered, every prayer made, and every offering given is a daily reminder that the conscience is disturbed. The daily trips to the temple and annual observances of specific Hindu holidays are constant reminders that neither last year nor the last 10 years nor an entire lifetime has been sufficient to bring lasting peace to the conscience. The concept of reincarnation simply acknowledges the fact that one lifetime is not long enough to be good enough. God uses the guilty conscience to silence any argument used to justify a person without Christ (Rom. 3:19-23).

The Calendar
History is moving in a specific direction, wielded by Someone great. Hindus approach history fatalistically; they believe the direction and control of history ultimately are out of their hands.

They consider the supernatural forces of *karma* and *dharma* to be the driving forces behind history.[16] To believe that history has a direction and meaning is to believe that Someone or something is directing it. The message of the calendar speaks of the love and providence of God and of His orchestration of the events of life. His providence demonstrates His mercy, but it also leads us to an encounter with God (2 Pet. 3:9). The reason why you are sharing the gospel with a person from a Hindu background is the goodness and providence of God to lead the person to repentance (Rom. 2:4).

The Cross

Ignorant of the righteousness that God demands, Hindus have sincerely strived but failed to obtain peace (Rom. 10:2-4). As prophesied, God sent His Son as the Deliverer of humankind. He became a human being so that He might redeem humankind that is spiritually dead in trespasses and sin (Gal. 4:4-5; Eph. 2:1-3). Jesus Christ, the Son of God, bore the wrath of God as the sin offering for the sin of humankind (2 Cor. 5:21).

Whoever turns from worshiping and serving idols to placing his or her faith in Christ can have peace with God (1 Thess. 1:9-10; Rom. 5:1-2). On the cross Jesus Christ completely and irrevocably satisfied all of the righteous demands of God—past, present, and future (John 19:30).

The Christ

When a person trusts Jesus Christ as Savior, God forgives him or her—sins past, present, and future—and credits that individual with the righteousness of Christ. Having the righteousness of Christ imputed to a believer allows God to consider that person as if he or she always had believed and obeyed like Christ. Salvation not only includes being justified by Christ but also being indwelled by the Spirit of Christ.

157

At the moment of salvation the Holy Spirit takes up residence in the believer (Rom. 5:10). As a believer yields to the indwelling Spirit, God is able to express His life in and through the life of that believer (Rom. 6:11-13). He becomes the believer's Life Source (Col. 3:3-4; Rom. 5:10).

Previously a person from a Hindu background was under the oppression of demonic activity. The fear of appeasing local spirits, demons, and ancestors surrounded the Hindu's life. But now in Christ that Hindu does not have a *spirit of fear; but of power, and of love, and of a sound mind* (2 Tim. 1:7) That new believer has Someone resident in him or her Who is greater than any person or thing in the world (1 John 4:4). By the Spirit of the Christ a believer has all that is necessary for living a godly life (2 Pet. 1:3-4).

The Coming

History is going in a direction and approaching a conclusion. Jesus Christ will return. The first time He was here not to condemn the people of the world but to die on the cross to provide salvation (John 3:17). His return will be to judge all peoples who presently stand in condemnation because of their unbelief (John 3:18-20). The intent of His mercy and patience is to provide an opportunity of repentance and faith before His return, because His return will be at an unexpected time (2 Pet. 3:9-10).

Jesus Christ is the only Way to God. He defines reality and is the Life Source of a believer's life (John 14:6). Therefore, salvation is found only in Christ (Acts 4:12; Mt. 1:21). Even a strict adherence to one's *dharma* is insufficient for a right standing before God because it is an attempt at righteousness that is established by the works of an individual instead of by faith in Christ (Rom. 10:2-4; Phil. 3:4-9). On that Day of Judgment only a believer who has trusted in Christ can have confidence because that person stands in the righteousness of Christ (1 John 4:17-18).

Communicating the gospel to a person of a Hindu background may take multiple conversations. These seven points are useful both for a presentation of the gospel and for knowing key talking points for discussing the gospel. Remember that a precise articulation of a method of sharing the gospel is not what gives a presentation power. Rather, a powerful witness occurs when an individual, full of the Holy Spirit, places complete confidence in the Holy Spirit to convict. Even the apostle Paul, who had a method of sharing the gospel, placed his confidence in the Holy Spirit to convict and save the lost (1 Cor. 2:1-5).

Questions/Issues Hindus Might Have

Again, as with the Buddhists, Hindus might not ask about your faith. Hindus can be very private about their religion. Many of these questions will overlap with the questions a Buddhist might ask.

1) Why can't I be a Hindu and a Christian at the same time?

Your response: Jesus said, "*I am the way, the truth and the life. No one comes to the Father except through me*" (John 14:6).

To follow Christ requires a total commitment to Him as a person. One cannot at the same time be a follower of Christ and of another form of salvation. Christ is the One who sets the standards of how He is to be followed. We are not the ones who set them.

2) Can you not believe in reincarnation? A cycle of life certainly seems apparent. Just look at the seasons of the year and the cycle of life and death; I believe a cycle of reincarnation must exist.

Your response: Christians do not believe in reincarnation but instead believe in resurrection. We believe that if you have given your life to Christ, on your death your spirit will be with God. If you have rejected His Son, it will be separated from Him. We believe that when He returns to judge us all, God will give us glorified bodies. The Bible teaches that we have one chance at this life; then we will face judgment (Heb. 9:27). However, for those who have given their lives to Christ, judgment is not something to dread but something to anticipate.

3) I think the idea of following only Jesus Christ is intolerant.

Your response: Something being intolerant is different from something being TRUE. Christ did not teach intolerance. He taught us to love our neighbors and to treat each other with respect. However, He also told us that the foundation for this love and respect occurs through Him. He is the basis of all Truth.

4) You say that Christ was here to free all people, but the world still has so much sadness in it.

Your response: Christ always spoke plainly to His followers about the realities of this world. He let us know that this world is broken with the reality of sin. The evil we do is real and damages our lives.

Evil and suffering are not in our imaginations; instead, they are very real. At some point you and I both have experienced true pain in this world. If you haven't yet, you will. No matter how much we meditate or try to do good deeds, this doesn't take away from the fact that we have true pain. Christ promises to give us abundant lives (John 10:10) and also to give us true relief from pain when we get to experience God for all eternity.

5) I do not believe we are all evil; we are born good.

Your response: Are you a parent? Do you teach a child to lie or be rebellious? Children inherently know how to do WRONG and must be taught how to do RIGHT. How do they know to do wrong? They know because they have been born with a sin nature. God allows us to be born into sin because He wants us to have two glorious gifts. The first of these gifts is freedom. This is the freedom to choose or not to choose to love Him. God does not force anyone to love Him. He wants our unconditional love and commitment. That occurs only as He gives us the freedom to choose to commit to Him. The second gift He wants us to have is the gift of grace. Only when we realize how far short we are to his perfection can we truly appreciate what a GIFT knowing Him is. We know Him in our sin because He first loved us.

6) The religion you describe seems to be one in which, under the guise of grace, you can do anything you want.

Your response: By no means can we do whatever we want. Giving our lives to Christ is an act of submission to Him. In other words we have the freedom to sin, but we choose to try to live upright lives because of what He has done for us. We choose to do right because we love Him and desire to live in obedience to His will, not because we are afraid of what He will do.

7) My duty is to fulfill my obligations in life to my family. I cannot necessarily change religions and forego my duties.

Your response: One of God's core commandments is to honor our fathers and mothers (Ex. 20:12). Christ also scolded people when they talked about doing good but forgot to take care of their parents (Mark 7:9-12). However, God also wants us to follow His plan for our lives. If we follow His plan, He will bless us eternally; this gives us an opportunity to bless others as well. What better way to give our parents the honor they deserve than to share with them the truth of how to know the One True God?

God bless you in your attempt to witness to your Hindu friends.

---

[1]Mandryk, Jason, *Operation World: The Definitive Prayer Guide to Every Nation* (Downers Grove, IL: Intervarsity Press, 2010), 2.

[2]*http://www.christianitytoday.com/ct/2011/july/indiagrassrootshtml?start=2*.Todd Johnson, director of Gordon-Conwell Theological Seminary's Center for the Study of Global Christianity, placed the number slightly lower at 58 million.

[3]Mandryk, *Operation World*, 407.

[4]Thirumalai, Madasamy, *Sharing Your Faith with a Hindu* (Minneapolis: Bethany House, 2002), 14.

[5]Thirumalai's work is a wonderful asset and should be in every believer's library. If you are looking for a far more in-depth study of Hinduism, please consult this work. This work also includes many Bible verses you can use in sharing your faith.

[6]Of course the Indian Jains, Sikhs, Muslims, and Christians that also reside in India might have some issues with that belief.

[7]Hexham, Irving, *Understanding World Religions: An Interdisciplinary Approach* (Grand Rapids: Zondervan, 2011), 139.

[8]Special thanks to Winfried Corduan for his help in the following sections. Without his guidance and correction I could not have written the following sections.

[9]Corduan, *Neighboring Faiths*, 202.

[10]Thirumulai, *How to Share Your Faith with a Hindu*, 57-58.

[11]Earhart, Byron, *Religious Traditions of the World* (San Francisco: HarperSan Francisco, 1983), 725.

[12]For security reasons Anjan's full name is being withheld.

[13]David S. Email interview, March 2012. For security reasons David's full name is not given.

[14]Charping, John. Email interview, February 2012.

[15]The points listed are adapted from John Chaping, *The Glory Story: Seeing God's Eternal Purpose,* 2012. Used by permission.

[16]The concept of time in Hinduism is cyclical compared to the linear concept of time in Western thought. Even within a cyclical concept of time, time is moving in a direction.

Chapter 9

How to Witness to Your Mormon Friends

Family oriented. Clean cut. Prominent in many political and economic circles. Fervent in faith. All-around nice folks.

I think these phrases accurately describe many Mormons. In so many ways one easily could assume that Mormons are just one more set of fervent Evangelicals. We tend to think that maybe the slight variations they have with Baptists, Methodists, Presbyterians, etc., aren't enough to make any real difference. After all, Mormons believe in God, Jesus, sin, church, and heaven. With all of those facts they've got to be Christians! If in numerous interviews Joel Osteen can proclaim that Mormons are Christian,[1] and he's the pastor of the largest church in the country, then Mormons must be OK . . . right?

According to Scripture, being nice, family oriented, clean-cut and fervent fulfills none of the requirements to be right before the Lord. Consequently we can respect Mormons (who call their body *The Church of Jesus Christ of Latter-day Saints*) for much of the way they live, but we also can accept that theological issues in the Mormon belief system are outside of what Scripture holds as sacred.

If you are like most believers in Christ, you are not aware of many details of Mormonism. Because of this fact, the background section of this chapter is an extremely important section—on par with the dialogue section. Why? Because to a Mormon the dialogue/witnessing section will sound very familiar. However, when you point out the differences in background beliefs between us and the Mormons, this can be quite a shock to them. Both their past history and their present core beliefs do not line up with mainline Christianity. The variations between Mormons and Evangelical Christians are not slight; they are utterly profound differences. In fact often the only commonality we have with Mormons lies in the words we use.

Mormonism–Background

The details of the beginnings of the Mormon church should give anyone pause.

The Mormon church began after a revelation occurred to a young man named Joseph Smith (1805-1844). In 1820 (note the young man's age), Smith received a vision from two personages that told him all denominations are wrong and that he should not join any of them. Those two personages were God the Father and God the Son. This vision did not immediately impact Smith's life; he did not discuss it in great detail until long after the Mormon church had started.

In 1823 the angel Moroni visited Smith and gave him two golden tablets. These tablets described the people that once lived in America. Smith claimed that these peoples were descendents of the Jews. According to Smith the tablets he received were written in ancient Egyptian. In 1827 Smith took the records and two stones, the Urim and Thummim, which helped him translate the records. Two other men also were allowed to see the golden plates. Also in 1827 Smith tried to join a local Methodist church[2] (a detail of which most Mormons are unaware).

In 1829 Smith and Oliver Cowery (one of the other men who had seen the golden tablets) were bestowed the keys to the Aaronic Priesthood and were prepared to establish a new church. By 1831 Smith planned to move his new church to Ohio but stopped in Independence, MO. By 1833 the Mormons were run out of the county. In 1835 Missouri allowed the Mormons to move to a new county. Also in that year, a key scripture among the Mormons, *Doctrine and Covenants*, was written. In 1838 grave financial losses caused 15 percent of Mormon adherents to leave the church, but the movement pressed on. However, division occurred among the people of the Mormon church; a riot occurred among the adherents. In the ensuing confusion a member of the Missouri militia was killed. In 1839 Joseph Smith consequently was placed in jail. At this time Smith began to teach on the plurality of gods, polygamy, and the need to baptize for the dead. By 1844 Smith was arrested and died in jail. Brigham Young took over the leadership of the majority of Mormons. He led the followers out West. Eventually the group arrived in Utah. With Utah as their home base of operations, Mormons grew into the formidable political and religious force they are today.

What Are the Differences Historically between Mormonism and Christianity?

What, if anything, is troublesome about the history of Mormonism?

1) An 1,800 year-old gap exists between Joseph Smith and the time of Christ and His apostles. All of that time the true church had been lost.

2) A 15-year-old boy received a message from an angel that told him all churches were apostate.

3) After this 15-year-old boy had an encounter with the angel, he still felt the need to defy the truth that all churches were apostate and decided to try to join a Methodist church.

4) The Scriptures needed to be translated from Egyptian. (Jesus and His disciples did not speak or write in Egyptian. No scholar holds that any book of the Old Testament

or New Testament was written in Egyptian). Consequently, Smith translated these Scriptures without having
ever studied Egyptian.

5) One of the core texts of the faith teaches that an entire
civilization of Jewish descendants was in America. No
archaeological evidence supports this claim.

Even with these apparent logical inconsistencies from the
Mormons' historical account, the theological differences between
Christianity and Mormonism should be sufficient reason to cause
concern for the Christian.

As previously stated Mormons and Christians have great sim-
ilarity in the terms they use. Mormons believe in God, Jesus,
heaven, and sin. However, how do Mormons define these terms?[3]
If you look at the Mormon church on a surface level, it sounds
like a typical Christian denomination.[4] However, one quickly understands that what Mormons mean when they use traditional
church vocabulary often is very different from the historical
meanings of the terms.

As one digs deeper into the definitions, the meaning becomes
more apparently divergent from those of Orthodox Christianity.
If a Mormon attempts to give you general definitions for the
terms below, you can ask whether these definitions more accurately reflect what the Mormons teach.

God—Mormons believe that God is the ruler of this planet.
However, he is only the ruler of this particular planet. He ac-
quired that status over a progression of time. He has a physical
body and flesh.[5]

The Bible, however, teaches about only One True God (Deut.
6:4-6). He is not one of many gods.

Jesus—In Mormonism, Jesus is God's son by a physical
union with Mary. Jesus, like God, was a human being but attained

godhead by living an upright life. He is the only person on earth to have a physical mother and an immortal father. He is the spirit brother of Satan. His death provides for the physical resurrection of all people. This doesn't mean that on death everyone will go to heaven, but everyone will have the right to resurrect.

The Bible teaches that Jesus always has existed (John 1:1) and is one with the Father (John 10:30). He was born of a virgin in a non-sexual union. He is far higher than the angels (Heb. 1), including Satan.

The Holy Spirit—Mormons believe the Holy Spirit does not have personhood in the Trinity as God and Jesus have. Instead, he is nothing more than a spirit manifestation that is from the Father.

The Bible teaches that the Holy Spirit is equal to the Father (Acts 5) and has personhood (Eph. 4:30) in the Trinity (Mt. 28:19-20).

Heaven—Mormons believe in levels in the afterlife. The highest heaven, *Celestial*, is reserved for those who have given their lives to Christ, as defined by the Mormon church. Another level of the afterlife, the *Telestial*, is reserved for Christians who have not accepted the Mormon approach to the gospel. This realm is not a place of eternal suffering, but it is not the highest heaven. Finally, Mormons believe in the *Terrestial Kingdom*. This is not hell, but it is a place for all of the unrighteous, immoral people of this world.

The Bible teaches of the existence of a literal heaven (Rev. 21) and a literal hell (Rev. 20). Heaven is reserved for those who have surrendered their lives to Christ, while hell is the abode for the devil, his demons, and all those who have rejected Christ.

Scriptures/Revelation—For the Mormon, the Bible is the word of God, but Mormons have three other Holy books: the *Pearl of Great Price*, *The Book of Mormon*, and *Doctrine and Covenants*. Also, each president of the church is seen as someone who can reveal new truth from God. His official word can be viewed as further revelation from God.

The Bible teaches that God has revealed Himself perfectly through His Son Jesus Christ. We also believe that He has given us His Word through the Old and New Testaments. The canon of Scripture is closed at this point (2 Tim. 3:16). The reason God allowed the canon of Scripture to continue past the Old Testament into the New was because of the arrival of the Messiah. Christ, through His Holy Spirit, enabled His disciples and those that had seen Him resurrected to write the New Testament (Eph. 2:20).

People—Christians believe that we are finite beings that are born with a sin nature, but we will live eternally with God the Father if we accept Christ as Lord and Savior. You and I have not eternally lived, but we will live for eternity in one of two places—heaven or hell.

The Mormon perception of humanity is quite different.

People are the preexisted spiritual offspring of the Heavenly Father and Mother. "All men and women are . . . literally the sons and daughters of Deity . . . Man, as a spirit, was begotten and born of heavenly parents, and reared to maturity in the eternal mansions of the Father, prior to coming upon the earth in a temporal (physical) body" (Joseph F. Smith, "The Origin of Man," Improvement Era, Nov. 1909, pp. 78,80, as quoted in GP, p. 11).They are born basically good and are "gods in embryo". A commonly quoted Mormon aphorism (attributed to fifth LDS president Lorenzo Snow) says, "As man is, God once was; as God is, man may become."[6]

For the reader, the fact that differences between the two churches are profound should be obvious. These are not minor differences. We are not debating peripheral issues that arise among denominations; these include worship styles, mode of baptism, or whether drinking alcohol is permissible. While important, none of those issues will prevent someone from knowing God. Mormons disagree with commonly held statements of theology that Christians have believed since the time of Christ. According to their texts they have "another gospel".

Even though this book contains a chapter about evangelizing Catholics and Protestants, I readily admit that in many aspects of theology Catholics and nominal Protestants are in agreement with Scripture. In no area do Mormons and Scripture have complete agreement. The two belief systems have fundamental differences. As a quick review Christians believe:

a. God was not once a person who BECAME God. Neither was Jesus. You and I CANNOT become God as Mormons teach.
b. You and I have not eternally existed as if we were gods.
c. Heaven and hell exist for those who have accepted or rejected Christ as opposed to the three levels Mormons espouse.
d. The canon of Scripture is closed. The only reason the Scriptural record was continued after the Old Testament to include the New Testament was because of the arrival of the Messiah and the apostles He appointed.

Mormons, in their attempt to portray themselves as exactly like biblical Christianity, have not painted a clear picture of who they are. At least Muslims, Hindus, or Buddhists openly admit their differences with Christians. In fairness we as Christians can cling to the hope that many Mormons do not truly understand the differences. One thing is for certain, however. Mormons are moral, kind, sincere people who are theologically completely antithetical to any version of orthodox Christianity.

The question becomes: how can I share my faith in a kind, loving manner with my Mormon friend or with the Mormon missionaries who arrive at my door when they do not recognize our significant differences?

Sharing Your Faith with Your Mormon Friends

As with all the other chapters, you can take four universal steps to beginning the process of sharing your faith with Mormons. They are:

1) Befriend them.
2) Avoid the urge to **just** be their friend and never engage in a spiritual conversation.
3) Look for the spiritual clues.
4) Seize the initiative even if spiritual clues do not present themselves.

For a detailed look at these four ideas, please refer to pages 33-37. Once you have taken a few moments to review these four steps, then you are ready to examine different approaches to talk with your Mormon friend. Here are a few approaches you could use:

The first approach to sharing your faith with a Mormon is from Shaun Payne. Payne is a converted Mormon who is pastor of a church in Memphis, TN. After he departed from the faith, Payne spent many years studying the Mormon church. Through the years he has witnessed to many Mormons. Most Mormons with whom he has interacted are missionaries. You can use Payne's approach with the missionaries that arrive at your door or with your Mormon friend across the street. Payne's approach, however, assumes you primarily are dealing with missionaries who are leading you through a study of Mormon thought.[7] You can use that study for an opportunity to share your faith.

Payne wrote:

Throughout the years, in my life God developed and culti-vated a great love for Mormons. Because of this, here are some ground rules for effectively sharing the gospel and displaying Jesus' image properly to those who practice the Mormon faith. More than likely, before you begin, you will have to eliminate some assumptions you have about Mormons. Before you share with a Mormon, please consider a few thoughts:

1) Not every Mormon is lost, but every Mormon is de-ceived. Mormons who have been in the church their en-tire lives will be more difficult to persuade because for their entire lives they have lived a lie. A new convert is more likely to see through the clear deceptions and con-tradictions.

2) Most Mormon men leave for two years to go on their "mission". A woman can go, but she is not encouraged to participate or condemned if she doesn't. Females typi-cally go for a year-and-a-half. A "mission" for Mormons means that they must save up enough money to support themselves for two years. Then they are sent to go and "make converts" in a context that is completely different from the place from which they originally hail. For ex-ample, men from the West of the United States will be sent either to the eastern section of the U.S. or overseas. This is done to help them learn what life is like apart from family, thus making them fully dependent on God. They are not supposed to watch TV, listen to radio, or partici-pate in other "worldly" activities. Instead they are ex-pected to study the book of Mormon, learn how to live their faith, serve those in the church, and evangelize out-side of the church. They have one day of rest in the week (in my experience, that day is Monday) in which they

hang out with other missionaries. When they return from their mission, they will get married and begin life. For this reason, we can assume that most men over the age of 25 we run across have left home and school for this mission of two years. Because of this I will focus on a means of evangelism I use with missionaries on their missions.

3) To share your faith, you will need to develop and cultivate a relationship that is built on humility and love for one who is deceived by Mormonism's false doctrines.

4) Thinking through the Mormon doctrine found on their websites and processing it is a good idea. This will help you to see some obvious contradictions from the Bible and the *Book of Mormon*. Utilize *Mormon.org* and *lds.org*.

5) Whatever you do, remember that all words about God, sin, etc., must be clarified and defined. We may use the same language, but remember that what we mean by these apparently simple terms is vastly different. Keep up with what is relevant in their belief system by following these websites.

6) Sharing the gospel is not difficult, but doing so will take some basic knowledge about what they believe combined with a little logic and a little hospitality.

Before They Arrive
1. Limit Distractions
Before they arrive seek to limit as many distractions as possible. Create an environment in which you can have genuine conversation. For example, if the television is on, turn it off before they enter. Because Mormons are not encouraged to watch television, a good rule is simply not have the television on when they arrive and while they are in your home. Begin to look around and

resolve things that you may perceive to be distracting. These may seem petty, but the goal is to limit any unnecessary distractions so conversation can flow easily.

If you plan to prepare dinner, have it ready and have the table as well as your living room clean. This will relieve anxiety on your part and enable both you and your friend to engage in heart-felt dialogue.

2. Know Their Language

Remind yourself that Mormons and Christians have very different meanings in the common words we use. This is why you need to use the following websites (*Mormon.org* and *lds.org*) and study the definition of the words you plan to use in your conversation.

3. Spend Time in Prayer

Because the point of the night is to fully expose Jesus and His gospel, spend time with Him. Too many witnessing experiences are absent from the Holy Spirit's power. Pray the Holy Spirit will give you grace to be able to be honest if they ask a question that you do not know. The temptation is to try to answer everything. Sometimes you just need to say you don't know. Understand that just because you do not know one answer does not discount the rest of what you do know.

At the Door

Know Their Typical Day

Remember that the typical day of a Mormon missionary involves going from house-to-house and meeting different people. Some of these people are terribly unkind. I personally have been out with some of the "missionaries". They endure a lot. They visit locations in which people clearly are home and act as if they are not. They have people slam the door in their faces or yell at them about how they are spreading the devil's work. They meet some well-meaning Christians who act as if the missionaries are completely without intelligence because they believe in the Mormon faith. I also have been with these guys as they go to the roughest parts of my city just to share their message.

Their day is long and exhausting. Along with evangelism, the missionaries are busy with ministries such as yard work, painting houses, etc., as they serve those in the church. Their days are incredibly packed. To have an offer for a free meal and a relaxed environment is a huge blessing. By showing interest in them we are not affirming what they do but rather are creating an environment for a gospel witness to occur.

Because of their typical day Mormons may expect you to act and do things in the same unkind way they have seen in others. Walk in the Holy Spirit so they will clearly see the gospel's effects in your life.

At the Table/Beginning the Witness

Have a good meal planned. We are cautious not to intentionally cause an offense for any Mormon. Mormons on mission are not encouraged to have caffeinated drinks. They also very rarely have a nice meal or have the opportunity to watch television. For this reason we deliberately serve water, enjoy a home-cooked meal, and focus on a great conversation to learn about each person's life and family. This is incredibly important, because during this time you will learn to whom and how to direct the conversation from this point forward. At this point you can begin with some questions:

1. "Where are you from?"

Again remember they are not accustomed to being treated with kindness,[8] they are not used to seeing a humble[9] Christian, and they are not used to being shown love.[10] Be intentional in establishing an atmosphere that is welcoming and loving. You are disarming them from any presuppositions they may have had as they entered the door.

2. "How long have you been out?"

With this question you are asking each missionary how many months they have been away from their home on this mission. This is important, because you are finding out which one has been out the longest. Because of this I always recommended engaging the one who has had less time on the mission field. You need to have a great amount of discernment here. The younger one may be more zealous and excited. He could be homesick, not enjoying his experience, etc. I focus on the one I believe I can cause a healthy amount of doubt in what he says he believes. I understand how that advice may sound to the reader, but that is what you want to do. You want the person to question what he believes so that he can honestly consider the Bible.

3. Next ask, "When did you begin to believe?"

I always ask about when they knew their faith was true. I ask about their family lives, people back home, job, school, and anything else I may find to be helpful in allowing me to know them better. I am also trying to understand whether their families can trace their linage back to Joseph Smith or whether they are converts.

4. Why Ask Questions?

One reason to ask questions is to have genuine interest in them as people. The other reason is to investigate how effectively to contextualize and communicate the true gospel.

Moving to the Living Room

After you finish your meal, move to a more comfortable environment. At this time the atmosphere should be a lot more relaxed and trusting. If they believe you really are interested in them—and because of the gospel, you should be—conversation naturally will occur. During their lesson questions can be asked easily. Let them begin their lesson about the Mormon faith. Give them the first word. I always get my KJV Bible out in an attempt to follow along. Remember, both Mormons and Christians use the KJV Bible.

Because of the vast amount of information that Mormons can use, I choose to focus on Joseph Smith's testimony as a young 14-year-old boy who was confused about the church altogether. The strategy of focusing on Smith is developed because you can show them that Joseph Smith, unlike Jesus, was a sinner and that he cannot be the Savior. If you can cause doubt in what Smith claimed, then they might find reason also to doubt the church he started. You don't have to directly claim he was wicked; just let His own words incriminate him as they openly contradict the Bible. Here is what to look for to expose their testimony:

In accordance with this, my determination to ask of God, I retired to the woods to make the attempt. It was on the morning of a beautiful, clear day, early in the spring of eighteen hundred and twenty. It was the first time in my life that I had made such an attempt, for amidst all my anxieties I had never as yet made the attempt to pray vocally.

After I had retired to the place where I had previously designed to go, having looked around me, and finding myself alone, I kneeled down and began to offer up the desires of my heart to God. I had scarcely done so, when immediately I was seized upon by some power which entirely overcame me, and had such an astonishing influence over me as to bind my tongue so that I could not speak. Thick darkness gathered around me, and it seemed to me for a time as if I were doomed to sudden destruction.

But, exerting all my powers to call upon God to deliver me out of the power of this enemy which had seized upon me, and at the very moment when I was ready to sink into despair and abandon myself to destruction—not to an imaginary ruin, but to the power of some actual being from the unseen world, who had such marvelous power as I had never before felt in any being—just at this moment of great alarm, I saw a pillar of light exactly over my head, above the brightness of the sun, which descended gradually until it fell upon me.

It no sooner appeared than I found myself delivered from the enemy which held me bound. When the light rested upon me I saw two Personages, whose brightness and glory defy all description, standing above me in the air. One of them spake unto me, calling me by name and said, pointing to the other—"This is My Beloved Son. Hear Him!"[11]

My object in going to inquire of the Lord was to know which of all the sects was right, that I might know which to join. No sooner, therefore, did I get possession of myself, so as to be able to speak, than I asked the Personages[12] who stood above me in the light, which of all the sects was right (for at this time it had never entered into my heart that all were wrong)—and which I should join. I was answered that I must join none of them, for they were all wrong; and the Personage who addressed me said that all their creeds were an abomination in his sight; that those professors were all corrupt; that "they draw near to me with their lips, but their hearts are far from me, they teach for doctrines the commandments of men, having a form of godliness, but they deny the power thereof."

He again forbade me to join with any of them; and many other things did he say unto me, which I cannot write at this time. When I came to myself again, I found myself lying on my back, looking up into heaven. When the light had departed, I had no strength; but soon recovering in some degree, I went home.[13]

(Payne wants you to read this passage before you set up the meeting. At this stage in your meeting, you still are allowing the Mormon missionaries time to go through their presentation.)

After they do their presentation, they will ask you to read and consider Moroni 10:3-5, which reads:

> *Behold, I would exhort you that when ye shall read these things, if it be wisdom in God that ye should read them, that ye would remember how merciful the Lord hath been unto the children of men, from the creation of Adam even down until the time that ye shall receive these things, and ponder it in your hearts.*
> *And when ye shall receive these things, I would exhort you that ye would ask God, the Eternal Father, in the name of Christ, if these things are not true; and if ye shall ask with a sincere heart, with real intent, having faith in Christ, he will manifest the truth of it unto you, by the power of the Holy Ghost.*
> *And by the power of the Holy Ghost ye may know the truth of all things.*

At this point ask whether they have read the Bible in its entirety. If the answer is "yes", then take them to particular verses that specifically deal with the issues presented with the testimony of Joseph Smith. I never have had anyone admit that he or she has read the Bible all the way through. Some have said they are "working through it". In kindness I share with them that no missionary should go out and proclaim a message that the person is not fully persuaded by or has not fully read. I share that telling people that the Holy Bible and the *Book of Mormon* are in harmony when in fact this is only an assumption is not morally honest. They have trusted someone else's testimony; so, therefore, their testimony actually is unacceptable. What if something you haven't read and studied in the Bible reveals that what you believe is directly in conflict to what the Mormon Church teaches?

Move from the table to the couch with the intention of allowing them to continue walking through their presentation. Be polite and respectful, so you will model listening; when you speak, you can ask for the same respect.

Listen as they walk through the first lesson. As you use Scripture to question what was just said, take notes, make appropriate observations, and interject questions. At some point in the conversation the following topics will arise. Included are some verses that help refute both Smith's and their own testimony.

Divinity of Jesus—Point them to the following passages which discuss who Christ and God are (John 1:18, 8:54-59; 2 Cor. 4:6; Heb. 1:3, Col. 1:15.) Explain that God is not a man (John 1:18). Explain that God is Spirit and our triune God is revealed in Jesus Himself. God is not compartmentalized or dispersed in three different beings but has chosen to reveal Himself through Jesus, Who always has existed.

"Another Gospel"—It is stated that the angel Moroni, who never is revealed in Scripture, was an angel God sent to be revealed to Joseph Smith:

> He said there was a book deposited, written upon gold plates, giving an account of the former inhabitants of this continent, and the source from whence they sprang. He also said that the fullness of the everlasting Gospel was contained in it, as delivered by the Savior to the ancient inhabitants;

179

Also, that there were two stones in silver bowls—and these stones, fastened to a breastplate, constituted what is called the Urim and Thummim—deposited with the plates; and the possession and use of these stones were what constituted "seers" in ancient or former times; and that God had prepared them for the purpose of translating the book.

Instead take them to Galatians 1:6-9, which warns us to flee from any gospel other than the one Scripture presents.

At this point share your testimony with your Mormon friends. Clearly present the gospel showing the clear difference between what they claim and what the Bible reveals. Show that the Mormon doctrine clearly contradicts the plain texts in Scripture. The goal is to open the Bible and expose, in general terms, the whole of the gospel beginning from Genesis 1 and ending in Revelation 22. This is the model that Jesus revealed (Luke 24:27; 44-49).

1. Creation—Genesis 1 (One God exists.)
2. The Fall—Genesis 3 (We fall short of His glory.)
3. Redemption—The Gospels: Matthew-John (God provided a remedy.)
4. Restoration—Salvation revealed: John 3:16 (God's salvation)
5. Culmination—the Kingdom fully revealed in heaven—Revelation 21-22 (Those who know Christ will get to go to heaven.)

You can use these chapters to give a brief overview of all of Scripture. In the process you can share the fundamentals of how to share your faith. If God leads, you can ask the missionaries whether at that moment they'd like to surrender their lives to Christ. This might be your only chance with these missionaries (or your friends, depending on the scenario). Take the opportunity to teach them how they can ask Christ to be Lord of their lives.

Out the Door

After the gospel is declared and displayed, you have a responsibility to try to continue and maintain a relationship so your life is not seen to contradict the gospel you just shared.

(Option #2)

Larry Green, a pastor in South Dakota, spent eight years in Brazil with the International Mission Board. Green brings a unique perspective to sharing his faith with Mormons. His approach also is directed more toward Mormon missionaries, but the steps can be used with any Mormon adherent.[14]

Please note the following truths:

1) Note how simple Green's approach is. You can learn his approach in a few minutes.

2) Note how Green focuses on one verse in Scripture (Rom. 10:9).

3) Note how Green searches for "folksy" illustrations to which everyone can relate. This is a key aspect of evangelism. If his illustration of Santa Claus is offensive to you, then choose an illustration that reveals how sincere individuals can believe in something and be sincerely wrong in the process.

4) Note how he gives the missionaries time to share their stories first.

5) Note his approach to witness to the more experienced missionary first, in direct contrast with Payne's earlier approach.

Green wrote:

While I attended seminary, I started witnessing to Mormon missionaries. I studied everything I could get my hands on for help to understand and present an effective gospel presentation to these young men. The problem I encountered was that most of the material at that time was very combative in nature and dealt mainly with the problems in the *Book of Mormon* and in their other writings. I felt as though I was in a maze of confusion and controversy that always ended up with my feeling as though I had won an argument, which made the Mormon missionaries ready to leave and never come back. This led me to ask whether I had done all I could to reach the young men for Christ and led me to find a different way to share with these missionaries.

As I got to know missionaries from repeated visits to my house, I noticed that I had much in common with them concerning how I felt about my family and the culture in which I was reared. My heritage and my family were very important to me; this also constructed my worldview before I became a Christian. The young missionaries in most cases were only 18- to 22-years-old; they had left home and family to reach a spiritual milestone in their lives. They had lived in Mormonism their whole lives and had watched and heard about how the generations before them suffered and sacrificed so that they could be here (ministering) today. These young guys had a lot riding on their shoulders. However, they were sure that their families had lived great lives before them and were indebted to their families as well as to Joseph Smith.

As I reflected on the sincerity of these missionaries, I'd like to give you a few things to remember, as well as some guidelines, when you minister to Mormon missionaries. First, they always arrive in pairs; normally one will be more experienced. Most books taught me to focus on the less-experienced guy in the pair. However, I never gave him any attention; I always focused and asked all questions to the veteran of the two. If I rattled or confused the lead guy, the other witnessed it and was influenced by it. (If at any time you raise doubt or confusion in their minds, they will send that missionary elsewhere to remove him from your influence. I saw this happen twice; both times the newer missionary was the one who got rattled.)

Second, they never will tell you where they stay or allow you to visit them. All of your interactions will be at your home or at a neutral site. These missionaries have supervisors in every city and daily check in with these supervisors. These men protect and watch the missionaries' progress. After a visit with me, I have had these supervisors phone me and ask me never to contact them again.

Third, they always have the same response when you ask whether you can use your own Bible. They respond, "We will use the King James Version, as it is translated correctly." They quote and know many Scriptures, but mainly they do this to disprove your faith and to bolster their belief in Mormonism. At this point I always take a pencil and paper and ask them to please write which verses are not translated correctly. They look at me with a blank stare, but to date I never have written down a single verse. The reason is that the Bible is not their main book and is very insignificant in their grand scheme. They make the above statement so that when they are cornered or can't explain something, they will say the Bible is written by people and contains mistakes.

Lastly, remember these are 18- to 22-year-old young men who have been trained to do this and have a manual that teaches them what to say and do. Maturity-wise they are no different than is any other college kid. Our goal is to get them out of the manual and routine that they have been trained to follow. We want them to think for themselves and to ask the question, "Could my parents and grandparents have been wrong?"

I always start the visit at my home. I tell the missionaries my children are my responsibility and will not be joining us at this time because I don't believe their gospel. I ask them how long the visit will take. They typically say about 30 minutes. I then ask whether I may have 15 minutes to share and ask questions after I give them 30 minutes of uninterrupted time.

You, as the reader, need to know what questions to ask, because these missionaries use the exact vocabulary as Evangelicals, but the words have different meanings. They will talk and get into their program about Mormonism and Joseph Smith. Everything for them revolves around your accepting that Joseph Smith was a prophet of God. Do not be offended by this tactic. He is the cornerstone of their faith; we want to talk about him. They will lead you right to him. In the end of their presentation, they will ask you whether you feel a burning in your bosom. They will ask whether you accept that Joseph Smith was a prophet of God.

At this point I ask questions. I always start by asking them to please share their testimonies. To be honest all Mormon testimonies sound the same: "I was a bad kid and didn't obey my parents." Typically you will hear very little talk about sin or God's grace. The fact is they almost all are baptized at 8-years old. (See *Book of Mormon*, Moroni 8:8-24; *Doctrine and Covenants* 29:46-47, 68:27) The church promotes and encourages this pattern.

As they give their testimonies, listen to how many times they say the name *Lord* or *Jesus*. They will say "Jesus", but the main gist of the testimony typically centers on, "I was a bad kid." I take note, because when I start to witness, I will tell them how many times they mentioned "Jesus" and "Lord". After they share their testimonies, I ask them whether they believe Romans 10:9-10. They say they do; I ask, "Is that what you did?" They always respond, "Yes." So I then ask again, "Does one have to confess Jesus is Lord and believe that God raised from Him the dead?"

Now armed with their testimony and acceptance of Romans 10:9-10, I ask, "May I have my 15 minutes?"

I ask them whether they are familiar with Joseph Smith's testimony. It is in the front of their *Book of Mormon*. They talk about it, smile, and share about his quest for which church was right. I ask them whether they find strange the fact that in his several-page testimony in the *Book of Mormon*, their prophet never confesses or even says Jesus is Lord. I remind them that in their own testimonies they called Christ "Lord" and confessed they were sinners or bad kids. I then point out how in Smith's testimony he talks a lot about himself, but not even once does he mention the name of Jesus. At this point they get mad, but I remind them that they told me I could have 15 minutes. I remind them that they just asked me to trust in a prophet who never calls Jesus His *Lord*. I then share my testimony with them. I also discuss the sinful state of humanity and the wonderful grace of Christ. For them to hear a sound Christian testimony is highly important. This is the most important thing you will do in this visit.

I close by asking them to show me in any of their writings— *Book of Mormon*, *Doctrine and Covenants,* or *Pearl of Great Price*—the point at which Joseph Smith said he was sinner in need of a savior. I also ask them whether they can show me where Smith calls Jesus "Christ" or "Lord." They spend a few minutes looking and talking but never find it. I respond by saying, "I am concerned that you have given your life to faith in a prophet that never has confessed that Jesus is Lord." I close by asking them whether when they were young, they celebrated Christmas and looked forward to Santa Claus. They say they did. I tell them how my mother and father and even my grandparents told me if I was good, Santa would visit me and bring me gifts. I explain how they knew it was not true but believed no harm could occur from the story. They knew that one day I would know Santa wasn't real. I tell them how one day at school a kid told me the straight of the story. I couldn't believe my family let me believe this. I look at the Mormons and tell them, "Guys, Christ is Lord; Joseph Smith is not a Prophet of God. I know your parents were and are great moral people, but your whole life they have steered you to trust in a man who wouldn't and never did call on the name of the Lord to be saved."

I then ask them if they would like to do what Joseph Smith never did and trust solely in Christ for forgiveness of sins and salvation.

Typically, they say "No!" I ask them to please return when they talk to their friends and supervisors and can show me the place in which their prophet confessed and believed in Christ. I can tell you I have seen some of these kids return for meals and listen to teaching about Christ. More than one time after our meetings the Mormons have removed some of the newer missionaries to other places. One of their bishops or handlers even told me never to speak to them again, but the sad truth is that I never have seen one saved in our visits. I can only hope that because I was faithful and shared Christ's sacrifice, love, and mercy, the strong hold of the evil one in Mormonism can be chipped away and that they will see the Light of the gospel.

Questions/Issues Mormons Might Have

1) How can you deny this experience that I have had? If you trust only the Spirit, you can't know the Truth as I have.

Your response: All experiences must be based on fact. You may have experienced something that felt as though it was an encounter with God, but does the truth of Scripture actually line up with what you believe?

2) Mormons are so fervent in our mission and so moral in our lifestyle. How can you deny that our faith is not valid?

Your response: I do not deny that you are sincere in your

faith, nor do I deny that you have some elements of truth to your faith. For example, you teach on morality and good works and maintain an emphasis on the eternal. Unquestionably you are seeking to know God. However, ultimately, the god that you worship has been defined by "writings" that occurred 1,800 years after Christ. Those writings do not line up with what Scripture says about God, Jesus, heaven, or the Bible.

3) We might define terms differently, but we all are Christians.

Your response: The question isn't whether we all fit the academic definition of a Christian. After all, the Moonies, Jehovah's Witnesses, and a variety of other groups academically would be defined under the Christian umbrella.

Biblically, we are defined as followers of Christ if we have surrendered to Jesus Christ as Lord as He defines Himself. He never was a person that became God, He is Christ that is both God and a human being.

4) Are you suggesting that Joseph Smith was a false prophet?

Your response: I never attack the founder of another belief system. I only ask you this: Do you find God's revealing Himself to a 15-year-old boy almost 1,800 years after Christ's ministry to be curious? What about the fact that an angel showed Smith that all of those believers before Smith's time had to be wrong? Doesn't that seem odd? If all these great men and women of faith from just after the first century until then were incorrect, doesn't that seem strange?

5) If you will just read our *Book of Mormon*, you will see the truth.

Your response: I think we should both read the book that we agree on. Why don't we both read the KJV Bible?

Also, if the *Book of Mormon* is the final revelation, does that mean the Bible is null and void? If that's the case, it suspends the argument that you are a Christian religion if our common Scripture isn't authoritative.

Why don't we sit down and study the Bible together and see what we can learn together? (If that's the case, take them through the Book of John.)

[1]*http://www.youtube.com/watch?v=IXYNqVdcgEI@feature=related* (accessed November 24, 2011).

[2]Many key facts in the historical overview are from former Midwestern Baptist Theological Seminary President Dr. Phil Roberts in his helpful work, *Mormonism Unmasked*.

[3]If the reader wants further study on how to define terms other religions and sects of Christianity use, the second chapter of Walter Martin's *Kingdom of the Cults* gives wonderful ideas that offer background information that helps in the dialogue with a multitude of religions.

[4]*http://mormon.org/jesus-christ/* (accessed November 27, 2011). A brief perusal of the website looks as though it could represent any Evangelical denomination's webpage.

[5]*http://www.4truth.net/fourtruthpdnew.aspx?pageid=8589952801*. The following definitions are based on wording from this helpful evangelistic website as well as from Roberts' book mentioned above.

[6]*http://www.4truth.net/fourtruthpdnew.aspx?pageid=8589952801*.

[7]Payne, Shaun. Email interview, February 2012.

[8]Romans 2:4, Colossians 3:12, Proverbs 11:17.

[9]Luke 14:11, Romans 12:3, James 4:10, Ephesians 4:2.

[10]Colossians 3:14, 1 John 3:18, Romans 13:10, Romans 5:8 (reflect on God's posture toward us while we were in conflict with Him.)

[11]Galatians 1:6-10.

[12]The personage never was clearly defined as Jesus or was even called by His name. In every resurrection account in Scripture Jesus always showed that He was the One being identified.

[13]*http://www.ids.org/library/display/0,4945,104-1-3-4,00.html*

[14]Green, Larry. Email interview, February 2012.

Chapter 10

How to Witness to Your Atheist/Humanist/Agnostic Friends

Initially, when I began to ponder writing this book, I assumed this last chapter would be about Jehovah's Witnesses. Although this denomination has significant numbers,[1] I believed that in this country another group was superseding the Witnesses. Most certainly people who fall in the "non-religious" category are having a larger societal impact, or at least a perceived grander impact, in the world today.

Whereas a few short years ago, you might not have wanted to mention a lack of belief in God in a public setting, that day has passed. According to *atheists.org*, 12 percent, or 37 million Americans, are atheists. This group claims to be the fastest-growing "segment" in the U.S. More atheists are in America than are Hindus, Buddhists, Muslims, and Jews COMBINED.[2] That means more atheists are in this country than are all the people who live in Canada.[3]

Lack of religious belief is far more than an American reality. *Adherents.com*, a popular website detailing religions of the world, states that "non-religious" individuals, which includes "agnostics, atheists, secular humanists or people that answered 'none' or no 'religious preference'", comprise 16 percent of the world's population. With statistics such as these, one might think that the age of a completely secular society is soon to be here.

Not so fast.

While some atheists have propagated the idea that they are greatly increasing in number (and to some degree, they are), other scholars hold a different perspective: "Nevertheless, atheists have represented only a small (if vocal) minority of Americans. Surveys estimate that atheists represent less than two percent of the population, even as the larger group of 'unaffiliated' includes over 15 percent."[4]

In truth on a national scale, the percentage of atheists hasn't increased since World War II. In fact, as a percentage, atheists actually have DECREASED from certain times in our history. According to a Gallup poll in 1947, 6 percent of the country claimed not to believe in God. By 1964 the number decreased to 3 percent. In 1994 it was 3 percent; by 2007 the number held at 4 percent. While since 20 years ago atheists have increased numerically, when one looks over a larger span of time, atheism has not grown as a percentage of our country.[5]

On a global scale, as a percentage of general populations, atheism still is statistically quite small. How small? Even in countries that Christian missions strategists long have shown to be very resistant to the gospel, the majority of the population of most countries still is very religious. For example, only 2 percent of the population of Austria, Taiwan, and Ireland claims to be atheists. In Italy, Iceland, and Finland only 3 percent claims no belief in God. In Canada, Switzerland, Greece, India, and Norway only 4 percent of the people are atheists. Finally in Denmark, Great Britain, Hungary, Albania, Greece, New Zealand, and Australia the numbers are 5 percent.

Former communist countries follow the same pattern. In fact, surprisingly countries that comprise the former Soviet bloc nations are surprisingly RELIGIOUS.

Russia is 4 percent atheistic, Ukraine is 3 percent, and Romania, Poland and Georgia are 1 percent. Considering what the church went through in many of these countries, one author best described the status of Christianity in Russia after so many years of political oppression of religion: "God 96 percent, atheism 4 percent—precisely the same as in the United States."[6]

So why do atheists seem to be so influential when their actual numbers are so small? First, atheism is in the mainstream of pop culture. At first atheism was an idea primarily bantered about in the academic world. However, with the very popular writings of Richard Dawkins, Daniel Dennett, and Christopher Hitchens, atheism is in the hands of the masses. People assume more atheists live in the West than actually do. Second, if we consider including other groups in the "non-religious" category—agnostics and secular humanists—the numbers do grow.[7]

This chapter focuses on three groups within this "non-religious" category. Those in the first group—*atheists*—are defined as those who do not believe in a higher power. *Atheists.org* said,

> Atheism is the lack of belief in a deity, which implies that nothing exists but natural phenomena (matter), that thought is a property or function of matter, and that death irreversibly and totally terminates individual organic units. This definition means that there are no forces, phenomena, or entities which exist outside of or apart from physical nature, or which transcend nature, or are "super" natural, nor can there be. Humankind is on its own.[8]

Happy thoughts, huh?

Those in the second group—*agnostics*—are people who are not sure about a higher power and reserve the right to not know for sure if he/she/it exists. Finally—*secular humanists*—may or may not be agnostics, but they hold to the preeminence of humanity and science over theology. In a sense, even if they pay lip-service to some belief in God, ultimately the highest authority in their lives is humanity and science.

What is the step-by-step process of sharing your faith with each of these groups?

In this chapter I propose a different approach. We will attempt to lump all three non-theistic groups together by their common denominator—the glorification of humanity. In the end, each elevates people to a higher degree than we deserve. Atheists don't believe in God, so consequently they seek out some type of higher authority in their lives. That highest authority might be government or science, but more often than not the atheists themselves will be the judge of right and wrong in their lives. The same pattern holds true with agnostics, although agnostics at least are humble enough to admit they could be wrong on the issue of theology. For the secular humanist, the world of science, professors in a given field, or once again secular humanists themselves will be the final authority in their lives.

Consequently, with each of these three, my approach would be to chip away at the armor of intellect by addressing the obvious problems of placing ourselves as the ultimate authority in our lives.

How Can I Share My Faith with an Atheist/Agnostic/Secular Humanist?

I suggest following the first four steps as outlined in the earlier chapters. For a more in-depth study of these four steps please see pages 33-37; 48-52 in the chapters on Catholicism and Protestantism.

1) Befriend them.
2) Avoid the urge to **just** be their friend and never engage in a spiritual conversation.
3) Look for the spiritual clues.
4) Seize the initiative even if spiritual clues do not present themselves.

With Step 4 keep two things in mind in particular. First, the typical atheist/agnostic/secular humanist highly values intellect. Even if the person isn't particularly intellectual, all people like to THINK they are intellectual.

For example, one of my old acquaintances who was in the beginning stages of entering the ministry informed me a few years ago that he now was an agnostic. He had read ONE of Hitchens' books and already had determined that he couldn't be a Christian anymore. Never mind the fact that in the early stages of any theological pursuit a student studies many books that actually address most of these attacks from these pop culture works.

The truth, however, was that my friend had read one book and probably would not take the time to read further on the subject, but he had made up his mind that he now was a thinking person and that he didn't need God anymore. Imagine this: One book and a couple of hours of reading, and he's out of the ministry. Why did he give up on God so quickly? The simple answer is found in point two.

Second, most people who give up on God this quickly do so because they want CONTROL. They might have some sin issue in their lives they want to continue practicing. They might have a pride issue that keeps them from taking direction from others. In this case my friend wanted to live life on his own terms and consequently determined that he no longer was sure about the validity of God. (Thankfully, years later he returned to the Lord.)

In light of these two factors, your bridge to the gospel might be a bit different from the approaches in other "religions".

When the time is right, you can ask the following leading questions:

(Option #1)
"(Friend's name), may I ask you a deep question? Do you feel as though life has any purpose?"

If the answer is "Yes," then ask, "What is the purpose?"

If the answer is "No," respond that you recognize that you might not have all the answers, but you think that life has a purpose.

(Option #2)

"(Friend's name), may I ask you a question? Would you define yourself as being *happy* or *joyful*?

Most people like to assume that they are happy. This type of question affirms that they are "happy". At this stage, you just need to build a bridge to explain your happiness.

If the friend responds, "I am neither", you can let the person know that you have "joy". Joy is true fulfillment even if you don't feel emotionally happy.

If the person responds "happy" or "joyful", you can share why you have joy.

(Option #3)

"(Friend's name), I know that you are well-studied. I try to study diligently myself. Can I ask you a tough question? Have you ever had a time in your life you have thought about God?"

This type of lead-in allows you to compliment the person's intelligence, but it shows you try to think through issues as well. Don't belittle another person's intelligence by beating around the bush. Go straight to the religious topic.

If the answer is, "Yes," ask "When?"

If the answer is, "No", ask whether the friend would mind sharing why he or she hasn't thought about God.

Regardless of what option you use to begin a witness:

If the friend gets defensive at this point with any of the three options, explain that you are not trying to be aggressive or too personal. Say that the friendship you share is important to you;

however, this is a topic that is central in your life and you just want to share about it.

If your friend allows you to continue, you can state:

"I know that now we have a hard time believing a lot of what we see. Nothing seems certain. I've always struggled with believing ANYTHING I hear. People have had that same struggle all through history.

"Something changed in my life, however. Somebody shared a story from the Bible with me that impacted my life. It's just a few verses; may I share them with you?"

If the answer is "Yes," then read John 18:28-38:

Then they led Jesus from Caiaphas to the Praetorium, and it was early morning. But they themselves did not go into the Praetorium, lest they should be defiled, but that they might eat the Passover. Pilate then went out to them and said, "What accusation do you bring against this Man?" They answered and said to him, "If He were not an evildoer, we would not have delivered Him up to you." Then Pilate said to them, "You take Him and judge Him according to your law." Therefore the Jews said to him, "It is not lawful for us to put anyone to death," that the saying of Jesus might be fulfilled which He spoke, signifying by what death He would die. Then Pilate entered the Praetorium again, called Jesus, and said to Him, "Are You the King of the Jews?" Jesus answered him, "Are you speaking for yourself about this, or did others tell you this concerning Me?" Pilate answered, "Am I a Jew? Your own nation and the chief priests have delivered You to me. What have You done?" Jesus answered, "My kingdom is not of this world. If My kingdom were of this world, My servants would fight, so that I should not be delivered to the Jews; but now My kingdom is not from here." Pilate therefore said to Him, "Are You a king then?" Jesus answered, "You say rightly that I am a king. For this cause I was born, and for this cause I have come into the world, that I should bear witness to the truth. Everyone who is of the truth hears My voice." Pilate said to Him, "What is truth?" And when he had said this, he went out again to the Jews, and said to them, "I find no fault in Him at all.

Now, explain the verses:

"Pilate couldn't help but ask, '*What is truth?*' After all, here was a good man telling him one thing, a group of religious leaders telling him another, and his own background in politics telling him something else. With everyone claiming to be right, Pilate had learned to doubt everything.

"The same thing happened to me in my life and in the lives of many of my friends. I read one article about a topic; it seemed right. I saw something else on TV; it seemed right. I heard a speaker on a different topic; it seemed right. Ultimately, I had begun to believe that no one was right. In the end, however, I started wondering if maybe at least ONE person was right. So I started to examine Christ."

At this point you may or may not want to give an opportunity to respond. You have not spoken for a great deal of time yet. However, your friend might be defensive about the name of Jesus. Take a minute more to explain your point.

Tell your friend, "I will be honest. After really examining Christ, I decided to give my life to Him. I cannot describe how much joy I have. I cannot describe how much more purpose I have in my life. Since you are my friend, I just want you to have those same things."

If your friend responds positively to this idea, then maybe you can push the situation a little further and explain how and why you gave your life to Christ. Use the following verses — Romans 3:23, 6:23, 5:8, 10:9, 10:13 — the same verses we have used for many of the religions we have studied. We use them because they give a clear, powerful, and simple presentation of the gospel. For further detail on how to use these verses see the chapters on Catholicism or Protestantism.

If your friend has some doubts about Christ being God but accepts that Christ, who was sent as a person just like us, might be a good thing for some people, then follow up by using C.S. Lewis' argument for Christ:

I know right now you might have doubts about Christ as being divine. However, I once heard a man describe Christ this way. Christ can be many things, but he can't just be a moral teacher. In fact he was either a liar, a lunatic, or the Lord. Christ claimed to be God (John 10:28-30). If He's not, He's a lunatic. He proclaimed to be the Truth (John 14:6). If He's not, He's a liar. However, if He claimed to be all of these things, and if all of it is true, then He must be Lord. He's the Lord of my life. I know this is very new to you, but . . ..

Would you please consider just thinking about what I've said to you today?"

The key fear you might have, as the Christian, is whether your friend will respond with difficult questions. If you want to field these questions, you can review the questions at the end of the chapter. However, never get into a debate with your friend about these lesser issues. Calmly respond as best you can. If you have questions, you always can ask your pastor how to answer them.

Witnessing Conversation Number 2

Joe Cadden has been in the ministry for more than 30 years. He has served the Lord in Maryland, Georgia, and Tennessee, and now is in South Carolina. He has shared his faith thousands of times and has extensive experience with people who do not believe in God. Growing up in the projects of Baltimore, Cadden has an extremely dysfunctional past. His past affects his witnessing style in the present. Cadden's approach is extremely unique; I believed it merited inclusion in this work. In fact, you could take Cadden's approach and use it with far, far more than just with atheists or agnostics. Cadden approaches a person by addressing inner pains of the past.[9]

You will be able to tell that Cadden's contribution is in a slightly different format from the others. This section reflects an interview I conducted with Cadden. However, I think readers will easily be able to adapt his style into their lives.

Witnessing by Viewing the Inner Pain of the Person

Author: Joe, how would you describe your witnessing style?

Joe: I never forget what it's like to be lost. For example I still can remember the taste of alcohol in my mouth from long before I knew I was a believer. It affects how I interact with a person who doesn't know Christ. Also, I expect lost people to act lost. For example, when Christians curse, that bothers me, but when lost people curse, it doesn't upset me at all. So when I go into a witnessing situation, I just talk. I don't try to be fake or super-spiritual.

Author: How do you begin?

Joe: Let me give you some tips on starting a conversation and keeping it going:

a) Be real: I try to just talk to people on a simple level about anything. I'll bring up sports, family, anything that might actually interest them—especially sports. People love to talk about sports. Remember, however: don't just talk about something that you don't really care about either. You have to want to talk to them on the topic. They can tell if you are faking it. I'll look for things that are real to talk about. Don't talk about the weather. Talk about their kids. They'll know if you are just trying to fill time. I remind myself that a liar knows a liar.

b) Be fair: After I've started the conversation, I want them to lead the conversation for a minute. Let them talk about what they want to. After all you ARE taking their time, so you need to give them time to lead as well.

c) Be prepared for biteback: Lost people aren't stupid— especially if you are a minister trying to talk to them about God. If they sense they might be about to be evangelized, they might start saying things to get you frustrated. They might discuss how church was bad to them in the past, or they might talk about a negative experience with a pastor. Let them even "taunt" you with things in their past. Don't let it bother you. Instead, let them expose those things that might have hurt them in the past.

d) Be kind: If a hurtful statement occurs, this is your moment to show them that you care. Let them talk. Show interest. I have found that at this point in the conversation you will probably have some lead-in to go to the gospel. You have been real with them; they can be real with you. They have shared their pain with you; you now can share Christ with them.

e) If you find a lead-in to the gospel, you don't necessarily go to Scripture. I don't whip out John 3:16. I'll say a passage from Scripture generally speaking—not word for word. For example I'll ask whether they've heard of John the Baptist. If they have (most of the time they have), I'll start with John the Baptist in John 3:30. Why John 3:30? The verse is so unique. Here's a guy (John the Baptist) that really served the Lord, but he ended up getting beheaded. Here is a man that has lived a very difficult life and tried to be good in doing what God called Him to do. However, in this verse he says that the purpose of his ministry was for Christ to increase and so he must decrease. It's an amazing statement.

I remind people that John the Baptist lost everything and went to jail innocently, but all he wanted to do was make Christ more in his life. The verse makes people think. I can transition to the fact that they might be having a tough life as well. However, I tell them that if Christ is real, and if everyone had that type of mentality that John did, wouldn't the world be a better place?

It's a great spiritual verse that doesn't look too spiritual. In other words I haven't gone into their sin yet or gotten too preachy. We're just talking about a guy who has had a rough life but still wanted to do the right thing.

f) At this point I'll give them time to share again about the pain they've been through. I let them just talk. Then I bring in John 3:16. I'll tell them about this verse. If they are sports fans, I'll talk about the guy that held up the John 3:16 sign at ball games. I'll tell them that even though people thought this guy was nuts, he endured embarrassment at times just because he wanted people to know there was SOMEONE (Christ) who cares about their pain.

g) At this moment I give my testimony. I tell them what Christ has done for me. I remind people that when I was a kid on the streets, everyone told me to "go to hell." No one ever told me to "go to heaven." In fact, even church people didn't tell me how to go to heaven. Sometimes they vaguely invited me, but most of the time I was just ignored. At this point people will jump in and say they "always" were invited to church or "never" invited to church.

h) I stress the idea that God loved and forgave me. This is a concept that boggles their minds. I remind them that I always figured my wife could love me and maybe forgive me unconditionally, but God Almighty? Why would He care about me?

i) I then take them to Daniel 1:8. It says, *But Daniel purposed in his heart that he would not defile himself.* I make them understand that to follow God requires commitment. I show them I decided that if God were going to love me, I was going to be committed to Him. (You can describe Daniel if you need to).

j) Finally, I take them to 2 Timothy 4:5. It says, *But you be watchful in all things, endure afflictions, do the work of an evangelist, fulfill your ministry.*

Why do I say this? This is one of the last things Paul says. He says it to a younger man that he has taught. He is teaching Timothy that God has given him a ministry. God has given my lost friends a ministry. They were created with a purpose. That ministry is in Christ. If they don't know their ministry, I'll guide them a little bit. For example I'll tell them that if they like people, then people are a ministry. If they say that they don't know what an evangelist is, I'll them it's not about preaching. It just means sharing what God is doing for you. What God did for you, He can do for anybody.

k) At this point, I ask them if they'd like to give their lives to Christ. I tell them they can say a prayer with me or without me. I stress the importance of the prayer. The only prayer He's going to hear is the one in which a person—any person—is calling out to Him. Christ can forgive my friends. The problem is, most people do not believe they can be forgiven. They might say, "You don't know what I've done." You can say, "I don't need to know: God already does and He still loves you." Let your friend know that God cares for the person. Show how to pray and give your life to Christ. Watch and see what happens next.

Witnessing Conversation Number 3

For many of us, trying to debate with a secular humanist is very difficult. How does one talk to someone who looks at the Bible and determines that it cannot be true because it doesn't coincide with science? This is the type of person with whom Mickey Rainey frequently deals. Mickey is a successful businessman who also is a bi-vocational pastor. For years in his spare time he has focused on studying philosophy and science to be able to reach the type of people God has called him to target. Currently, Mickey is a church planter targeting a very upper-class neighborhood in Memphis. This area is comprised of intellectuals from all over the country; they are there to work in nearby research institutions, hospitals, and universities.

The ensuing conversation represents a typical conversation he might have. Notice, as you read, that Mickey's goal is to establish the Bible as valid. He targets how the Bible is scientifically sound. He also points people to the core issue of why they don't want to believe the Bible. If it is true, then they must deal with areas of their lives that might be outside of what God has planned.

Read Mickey's conversation. Copying this exactly in real life will be difficult, but it should give you some ideas of what kind of pattern you could follow with your friends.

Carl: Ask Chris; I bet he knows
Chris: Ask me what?
Carl: Where to find Market Community Church, the one downtown.

Chris: Yeah, I know about where it is. I have a buddy who goes there. He really likes; you guys thinking about going? If you like, I could have him give you a call to show you around.

Carl: Mark is going.

Mark: Well . . . just for a funeral.

Chris: Oh, I'm sorry to hear that. Was the person someone close?

Mark: My uncle . . . my dad's brother. He passed this weekend. I wasn't real close to him, but my dad is having a tough time with it. I wish I knew something I could say.

Chris: You said the funeral was at the church? I hope you don't mind my asking, but was your uncle a Christian?

Mark: Yeah, their whole family has gone to that church since I was a kid.

Carl: And you don't know how to get there?

Mark: Their family went, not ours.

Chris: If it helps at all, I really believe that if your uncle was a Christian, you can say something that might comfort your dad. It sounds like your uncle believed that, too.

Mark: I guess you're right; he lived a good life. He was a good man.

Chris: Well, I'm sure he was, but that isn't really what I meant. As a Christian, your uncle would have believed in the promise that when his body died, he would keep living forever with God.

Carl: I would say that he lives on through all of us—his influence, his legacy, our memories . . ..

Chris: Not to press the issue, but I am talking about your uncle as a person living forever beyond the life of his body—not just the idea or memory of him, but the real person.

Mark: No offense, but I am not sure I buy into the whole life-after-death thing. Don't get me wrong; I think it's great if going to church helps people. I think we all have a spiritual side. I am not even saying some kind of god is not out there, but who's to say which religion is right, if any?

Chris: I agree that those are big questions, but I also believe they can be answered. I can certainly understand how someone could believe that God and spiritual things can be mysterious, but that doesn't mean that God isn't knowable. This is what Christians find so exciting about the Bible. The Bible is God revealing Himself to His creation. It's how we know what's expected of us, what's acceptable, and even what God is like.

Carl: If God exists, what makes Christians sure their book is right . . . or that any book is right? Reasonably, aren't these just philosophies and stories that became part of some religious tradition?

Chris: When I was in my undergrad years, I asked the same questions. I already was involved in church, but I had some real doubts that I wanted to work through. This question of the reliability of the Bible turned out to be one of the key questions. If you accept that the Bible is reliable, the essentials of the Christian faith are pretty clear. Ultimately, I was genuinely convinced that the Bible was what it claimed to be—a revelation from God.

Mark: Surely you understand that this is tough to swallow for some folks. I am no Bible scholar by any means, but I know it does teach a lot about miracles, the whole dividing of the Red Sea thing, virgin birth, and people being raised from the dead.

Carl: Seriously, Chris, I think most honest adults would agree that the Bible teaches things that have been proven to be false by modern science.

Chris: Hey, I get it. If the Bible teaches things that are proven false about a world we can see and touch, then how can we rely on it to describe a spirit world that we can't see? That is exactly what I struggled with. But as I worked through those issues, I began to realize that the Bible doesn't teach things that are false, including what it teaches about our world. Many of my struggles originated with people that made claims that went well beyond what the Bible actually taught. In fact, the more I studied what the Bible and science had to say about our universe, I was amazed at how accurately these ancient writers described what science has discovered in the last 100 years.

Carl: Give me a specific example.

Chris: OK. Let's start at the start. Would you agree that modern science understands that both space and time originated at a given moment in the past and have been expanding since that time?

Carl: Well sure, but the Bible teaches that God snapped his fingers and here we are. What does that prove?

Chris: Actually, the Bible teaches some very specific things about creation. I'll be quick, but let me give you three specific examples from the Bible:

1. First it teaches that time had a beginning. The first verse of the Bible says, *In the beginning . . .* or to be even more specific, a verse in 1 Corinthians says: *. . . we declare God's wisdom, a mystery that has been hidden and that God destined for our glory before time began.* Show me another writer before George Lemaitre that suggested a beginning for time itself.

2. Second example: the Bible teaches that the universe was stretched or expanded by God's hand. *He stretches*

out the heavens like a curtain, and spreads them out like a tent to dwell in. That is a verse in Isaiah 40, but it isn't the only one. In fact, this idea of stretching or expanding is the most popular picture in Scripture across multiple writers to describe the act of creation.

3. Even the simple idea that the earth is round would be unimaginable for an ancient writer. Biblical writers Isaiah and Solomon both spoke of the *circle of the earth.* In contrast, other writers of the same period were talking about pushing their enemies off the edge of the earth into space.

These are only a few examples. Thousands of verses in the Bible show how these ancient writers were able to speak with a vision far beyond themselves and their time in history. Not only are their writings accurate about natural history, but the same can be said for great insights to human nature, political history, and more. It's really pretty amazing.

Carl, earlier you said that the Bible teaches things that are aren't accurate. Did you have something specific in mind?

Carl: I can't quote the exact verse like you can, but I know that it teaches plenty of things that don't sync up with what we know today.

Chris: I would challenge you to find specific examples. I know when I did the same type of search, I was surprised at how much of what I was told about the Bible wasn't accurate.

Mark: So, obviously you believe all of this now. What ultimately convinced you that this was all true?

Chris: Well, like I said, as I worked my way through my list of doubts, I was pretty amazed at how well the Bible described not only the world we live in, but me as a person. I kept waiting to find some verse that made some crazy claim, but I never found it. One day I was mentally updating my doubt list. It wasn't completely cleared, but the issues were getting smaller in number and relevance. I'm glad that I made the effort to work through my doubts, but it didn't make me a Christian. It was something different.

Finally, I realized that my hesitancy wasn't about whether the Bible was reliable anymore. Things had started that way and I still had some open questions, but now my hesitancy was about me. I knew that if I accepted the Bible as true, I would have to deal with how I was living my life. I really didn't want to do that.

On the outside I was always seen as the kind of "goody-two-shoes" guy that others would ask for directions to a church (grin), but like everyone else in this world, my nature is to be selfish and live life my way. Answering my objections helped me consider the Bible, but accepting the teachings of the Bible is something different.

If you are interested, I would be happy to do my best to answer any questions you have about how the Bible was written, compiled, and kept accurate over thousands of years. These types of questions all have answers backed by physical proof. But ultimately I would love to show you what the Bible teaches about life after death, about who God is, and about how we can know Him. I think you might be surprised.

Carl: Guys, I hate to interrupt, but I gotta run, Mark, sorry again about your uncle.

Mark: I have to run, too. Sorry to keep you so long.

Chris: No trouble at all. I enjoy talking about this kind of thing. Mark, I didn't know your uncle, but I do know what they teach at his church. Life after death isn't about living the right way to earn your way to heaven. It isn't about hoping for the best. You sound as though you have an interest in spiritual things; at least make sure you understand what the Bible teaches about God and eternal life before you reject it. If you are interested, I would love to take you to lunch and go through it.

Questions Your Atheist/Humanist/Agnostic Friends May Ask

1) I know you believe that Jesus is God. I have heard that Jesus never claimed to be God. Is that true?

Your response: Of course Jesus claimed to be God. Jesus accepted praise and worship—something only God can do (John 1:49). Jesus changed water into wine, which proved He had power over the elements (John 2). Jesus claimed to be able to give eternal life—a gift only God can give (John 3:16). Jesus told people to break the Sabbath. Only God could claim authority to break His laws. Jesus claimed that He and the Father are One (John 10:27-30). I just gave you several examples; those are just from one book. Let's meet again so I can show you in the other Gospels other examples of Jesus claiming to be divine.

2) Most Christians are just not intellectual. In fact, Ted Turner said that Christianity was a religion for losers. Why would I want to be associated with that group?

Your response: Are George Bush or Barack Obama unintelligent? How about Martin Luther King or Bishop Desmond Tutu? Are they uninformed? In fact, throughout history hundreds of millions of people have been both believers and intelligent. Galileo was a believer. Einstein, though he never became a Christian, saw a divine hand in the process of the universe.

3) Hasn't Christianity brought nothing but pain and misery in this world?

Your response: The Bible teaches that we are to have love,

joy, peace, patience, kindness, goodness, gentleness, and self-control (Gal. 2:22-23). The essence of the Bible is to teach the good of this world. Occasionally people use it for bad purposes. Yes, people that called themselves *"Christians"* participated in the Crusades (which was more politically motivated than religiously motivated) and the Salem Witch Trials (which involved one demented pastor who quickly was denounced by his fellow clergymembers). However, we shouldn't discount the vast accomplishments for the good of this world that have occurred from people who followed Christ's principles.

4) What is one good thing that has occurred because of Jesus?

Your response: Slavery has occurred throughout the world and throughout history. Only after Christians in England stood and fought for slaves' rights did the practice end in the West. Women in the Middle East had few freedoms until Christ began to show the world their equality. Many of the freedoms that we assume in our daily lives in the West would not have occurred without Christ.

5) Do you not believe in science?

Your response: Why does a Christian not have to believe in science? We believe that God is the author of science. We think Christians should study the sciences thoroughly.

Christians recognize the importance of scientific facts. No one denies that "for every action there is an equal and opposite reaction" or that "2+2=4." However, Christians believe that God ordained those facts to be true. They view science as a way of glorifying the Creator through His creation.

6) What about all of the problems in the Bible?

Your response: My pastor showed me that almost every one of those "problems" in the Bible is very easily shown to be a misunderstanding in our reading. People genuinely debate very few passages. The debated passages still do not interfere with the core truths of Scripture—Christ died for our sins, He was buried, and three days later He rose again according to the Scriptures (1 Cor. 15:1-3).

7) What about evolution?

Your response: First of all, Christians express a great diversity of opinion about evolution. Secondly, according to a recent poll, only 39 percent of Americans definitely say they believe in evolution.[10] Maybe they all are wrong, but can we not even discuss the opinion of 61 percent of the people in this country? Can we possibly have some disagreement on this issue? I can give you the benefit of the doubt in your belief system, but can you be tolerant (use that word—*tolerant*) of the fact that I have some questions about evolution?

8) Isn't religion only a means of manipulating people?

Your response: I guess if something manipulates people to reflect once a week on "loving one's spouse", "loving my neighbor as myself", and "doing good to others", that's a pretty good manipulation! Actually, God's truths about day-to-day living affect all people, whether they are in church or not. Your moral compass has been defined by the fact that you have been reared in a "Christian" society—a society in which human life is valued, in which dissension is accepted without total persecution, and in which the basic tenets of the Ten Commandments are followed as the rule of law whether we verbally agree with them. If it's about "manipulation", whether we like to admit or not, we all are manipulated somewhat by religion.

9) Why should I be interested in Christianity? So many big-name Christian leaders are hypocrites.

Your response: You're right. In the Bible Jesus says we will encounter people who put on Christianity as a guise for their own true motives (Mt. 7). He tells us that by their fruit we will know the true followers of Christ. On this issue you and Jesus completely agree!

I join the millions of sincere believers who become frustrated with some of the evangelists, pastors, and other Christian leaders that act inappropriately—sexually and financially. God isn't honored by this. In the end I can tell you only that Christ is far different than what you might see portrayed on the television. I also can tell you that for every disappointing high-profile Christian are thousands of devout believers quietly trying to change lives through Christ. They will never be known except by the people they help.

By the way, I'd like to mention one more hypocrite—myself. This past week I'm sure I've (name your sins here). Daily we all fall short. Even those big-name pastors can recognize their shortcomings, repent of their sins, and still make an impact for God.

Throughout His ministry Christ taught the principle of grace. Even though we were still sinners, Christ died for us (Rom. 6:23). I'm not asking you to consider a religion in which you have to be perfect (although you should strive to act right). I'm asking you to consider a relationship with the One True God who by grace wants you to know Him.

May God bless you as you attempt to win your non-religious friends to Christ.

[1]http://www.watchtower.org/e/statistics/worldwide report.htm (accessed November 21, 2011). According to the Jehovah's Witnesses official website, JW meeting houses had 2,485,231 publishers (active members).

[2]Statistics are taken from atheists.org homepage. Note the professionalism of their website and the upbeat, friendly manner in which they promote atheism.

[3]Taken individually, more atheists live in America than the number of people who live in Uganda, Saudi Arabia, or the Sudan. We wouldn't even pause to think about sending missionaries to these important countries, with each having a population of between 20 to 40 million people. However, we often turn a blind eye to the 37 million atheists in our own country.

[4]Mohler, Albert, Atheism Remix: A Christian Confronts the New Atheists (Wheaton, IL: Crossway, 2008), 11.

[5]Stark, Rodney, What Americans Really Believe, 2008, 117.

[6]Ibid., 118.

[7]*http://www.adherents.com/rel_USA.html#religions* (accessed February 25, 2012). Taken from a survey of 50,000 people, the ARIS (American Religious Identity Survey) claimed that atheists were .4 percent of the population of America, agnostics were .5 percent, and people who claimed to be non-religious or secular were 13.2 percent of the population. Note the discrepancy between some sources that say atheists are four percent of the populace and .4 percent in other surveys. The differences probably are because of definition of terms. In the end people in the "non-religious" category still comprise about 14 to 15 percent of the United States.

[8]*http://www.atheists.org/atheism* (accessed Dec. 21, 2011).

[9]Cadden, Joe. Telephone interview, January 2012.

[10]*http://www.gallup.com/poll/114544/darwin-birthday-believe-evolution.aspx*

Appendix 1

What if I Don't Lead My Friends to Christ? Have I Failed?

Your success in sharing your faith does not depend on leading your friends to Christ. I'm aware that reading that statement can be difficult to believe. It feels almost like verbal spin similar to when someone tells us that "as long as we try, we succeed."

In this instance, statements such as "you cannot fail" actually are true. Christ is the author of salvation (Heb. 12:2). The Holy Spirit reveals all truth and convicts of sin, righteousness, and judgment (John 16:8). Ultimately, we are called to be ambassadors of the King who has delivered a message. He is the One who has to convict our hearts of the need for salvation. You and I are just the messengers—that's it. If we deliver the gospel accurately by relaying the three core truths that Christ died, was buried, and rose again (1 Cor. 15:1-4), then we have succeeded.

This does not mean that we shouldn't be well-prepared. Paul called himself a *master builder* in the faith (1 Cor. 3:10). Why could he say he was a *master builder*? Was Paul being arrogant? Actually Paul simply was pointing out that he was very well-prepared to do the task God had given him.

In like manner this book is designed to help you be prepared for a comfortable and authentic interaction with your friend. You can present the gospel in a kind, loving way because we serve a kind and loving God. How we present the gospel reflects how we feel about our God. If we view God as judgmental and mean, we will speak with a judgmental and mean tone. If we believe God is compassionate and loving, we will reflect Him in like manner. After you read this book, be prepared to plant the seeds of the gospel in your friend's life. However, more often than not, more than one attempt at sharing one's faith is necessary before a person converts.

One means that missions professors use to show the progression of evangelism among a people is the Engel Scale. The Engel Scale was created by James F. Engel, retired distinguished professor in the graduate programs at Eastern University and founder of the Center for Organizational Excellence.[1] Engel designed the scale to reflect the step-by-step process usually necessary for someone to profess faith in Christ. Sometimes people trust Christ the first time they hear the gospel. The norm, however, is for people to go through a series of decisions before they are ready to surrender to Christ. Although the scale is not perfect, and I have seen the wording change depending on the resource, the scale is a reminder of the process of salvation.

Note the process Engel describes. People can start out very far from the gospel truth (-10); or initially in the process they can be further along spiritually (-6). Your function is not necessarily to take a nonbeliever from a -7 (interest in Christianity) to a 0 (repentance and faith). Instead, your job is to share your faith and to be part of the person's journey as he or she travels step-by-step until the person reaches +5 (effective at sharing one's own faith).

Sometimes when I share my faith, the other person doesn't profess Christ at that moment; however, God uses me to take my friend one step closer to salvation. In light of this I know that the witnessing attempt bore fruit—even without a "visible" result. We seem to be shocked or disappointed when an atheist or Buddhist to whom we witness for 15-45 minutes doesn't surrender to Christ. This mindset is illogical. After all, did you give your life to Christ the first time you heard the gospel? Some of you may have, but for most the answer is "no." A process was necessary to help you know Christ. In the same way a process is required to help your friend to know Him as well. Rejoice in the fact that you get to be a part of His gradual plan.

Look at the scale.[2] Remind yourself that your function may be to lead someone to Christ today, but it also may be to inch your friend one step closer to the Truth about Jesus. Both steps are victories.

---

[1] *http://www.ivpress.com/cgi-ivpress/author.pl/author_id=1015.*
[2] Engel Scale diagram is found at the following address: *http://www.ywamcampaigns.org/Articles/100067091/Impact_World_Tour/Impact_World_Tour/Teaching/The /Engel/Scale.aspx*

simplified
Engel Scale

-10	No God framework
-9	Experience of emptiness
-8	Vague awareness of Christianity
-7	Interest in Christianity
-6	Awareness of the gospel
-5	Positive attitudes to the gospel
-4	Experience of Christian love
-3	Awareness of personal need
-2	Grasp of implications of the gospel
-1	Challenge to respond personally
0	Repentance and faith
+1	Evaluation of the decision
+2	Learning the basics of the Christian life
+3	Functioning member of local church
+4	Continuing growth in character, lifestyle, service
+5	Effective sharing of faith and life

Appendix 2

This Book Is about Witnessing to Friends. What about Family?

Of course the Lord wants us to witness to family as well as to friends. The Bible has ready examples of the gospel flowing along family lines (Acts 16:31).

I advise using the same techniques with family that this book has highlighted for friends. After all, if you live in the West, you probably have someone in your family that has dabbled in nominal Protestantism, Catholicism, Secular Humanism, and/or something else featured here.

However, people often hesitate to witness to family because family members "know" us. For years they've seen us "warts and all". Here is my two-part advice for witnessing to your family.

First, if you have given your life to Christ and have tried to follow Him for some time, or you have made an evident attempt to have life change, I STRONGLY encourage you to begin the process of sharing with family members. Being able to witness to your family should not be a hardship but actually is an advantage. Yes, they know all your foibles. However, they also LOVE you already. Many times that love gives you an open door to at least initiate a conversation. If you preface the subject correctly, grandmas, uncles, and cousins will give their relatives a hearing.

If you are looking for an opening to share, try something such as this: "Uncle John, I know I haven't been perfect in life, but something happened to me that really is important. Can I talk to you for about 10 minutes about this?"

If the loved one responds aggressively or appears uncomfortable, then say, "Something about Christ finally clicked with me. I do NOT want to preach to you. I just (love/respect) you and want to tell you what happened." (Some might rather hear you say *respect you* while others might want to hear you say *love you*. Hopefully, both are true.)

Is that a guarantee of acceptance? No. However, often we overanalyze sharing with our family. In fact, most of the time, Satan uses our overanalysis as excuse to immobilize us both with our friends and our family. Satan may whisper: "You can't say anything about Christ. They don't want to hear it. You'll embarrass yourself." Perhaps the most common voice you hear in your head is: "They'll never talk to you again. You'll close the door forever. Just seeing your life is enough."

I've shared my faith with several family members. Each time I've been nervous. However, afterward I've also been glad that I was obedient to God's prompting. For example, years ago the Lord laid on my heart the need for me to share with one of my cousins. The exchange went well, but she in no way was ready to respond to the gospel. Several years later, while I was on the mission field, she trusted Jesus and became a core member of our community's church. Did she get saved because of my witness? No. Did the Lord use me in her step-by-step process to begin to know Him? I believe so. Results with family might not be immediate, but they certainly can be rewarding.

Second, examine whether you personally have experienced life change. If you are at church on Sunday but booze it up on Friday, run around on your mate, or practice dishonest work habits, your family knows that. A good witness might involve waiting until you've exhibited evidence that Christ has changed you. In fact, if your walk shows no evidence of God and your lifestyle exudes sin, consider examining your own salvation.

I certainly don't imply that you must be perfect before you witness to your loved ones. No one expects this. They know that is impossible. By the fact that you have TRIED to live for Christ, you will have a more ready hearing than you probably expect.

Appendix 3

What if the Conversations Don't Follow Exactly as the Ones in the Book Do?

I have a simple answer for you: they often won't. Diversions from the pattern we have given you always will occur, because in this world everyone is different.

Some chapters deliberately are designed to try to cover all of the range of possible responses from a person (Catholic and Protestant). All of the chapters try to give you authentic, real-world conversations from which you can draw from the experience of others' evangelism techniques. My hope and prayer is that you read these conversations, pick up the patterns given, and then follow them as best you can.

Notice what most of these evangelists did in their approaches. They looked for a person's need, made a transition statement (bridge) to the gospel by showing how Christ met that need, and then, using their testimony and a few key verses, shared their faith. Time and time again I was struck by how the same pattern continually was used.

However, you still might be thinking: what if I get lost because we are not following the script? Here are two last pieces of advice:

1) Remember to direct the conversation. Give your friend time to express inner thoughts and struggles. However, at a certain point, take a deep breath and share the gospel with confidence. It's the BEST news the person ever will hear.

2) If you absolutely get lost (and we've all been there), redirect the conversation to John 3:16. Tell your friend that you are not a great theologian, but based on the verse you know that:

a) *God so loved the World*—that love includes you and your friend.

b) *He gave His only begotten Son*—He sent Jesus to Earth to live as a human being.

c) *Whoever believes in Him*—You personally already have put your trust in Christ. You believe that He died on the cross, was buried, and three days later rose from the grave (1 Cor. 15:1-4).

d) *Should not perish but have everlasting life*—Because you have put your trust in Him, the Bible promises that you will live forever with the One True God. Anyone who trusts in Christ can have that same confidence of eternal life.

You love and respect your friend. You want this person to have the same joy that you have. You even are willing to risk the friendship by talking about your faith simply because you care for this individual. Make sure you disclose WHY you shared about your faith in Christ. Finish with HOW the friend can pray and receive Christ.

That's it. If you get stuck, go to John 3:16. The gospel has power in it. Simply explaining that Christ died, was buried, and three days later rose from the grave is the core of the gospel. We often think we have to make a witness more complicated than it is. We need merely to let the gospel speak for itself. Let God penetrate your friend's heart. Paul understood the simple power of the gospel. We would do well to remember these simple verses in Romans 1: *For I am not ashamed of the gospel of Christ, for it is the power of God to salvation for everyone who believes, for the Jew first and also for the Greek. For in it the righteousness of God is revealed from faith to faith; as it is written, "The just shall live by faith."*

God bless you, my friend.

Additional Books for Further Study/Bibliography

Included is a brief bibliography of books and Internet sources for your further study. This list is not all-inclusive, but I have tried to include the most helpful sources. Interviews with my colleagues are not included in this abbreviated bibliography.

Akins, Wade. *Sharing Your Faith with Muslims*. Garland, TX: Hannibal Books, 2011.

Armstrong, John H. *Roman Catholicism*. Chicago: Moody, 1994.

Blackaby, Henry. *Experiencing God*. Nashville: B&H Publishing Group, 2008.

Braswell, George W. Jr. *Islam: Its Prophet, Peoples, Politics, and Power*. Nashville: Broadman & Holman, 1996.

Charping, John. *The Glory Story: Seeing God's Eternal Purpose*, 2012. Used by permission.

Corduan, Winfried. *A Christian Introduction to World Religions: Neighboring Faiths*. Downers Grove: IVP, 1998.

Earhart, H. Byron, ed. *Religious Traditions of the World*. San Francisco: HarperCollins, 1993.

Geisler, Norman L., and Abdul Saleeb. *Answering Islam: The Crescent in the Light of the Cross*. 2nd ed. Grand Rapids: Baker, 2002.

Hexham, Irving. *Understanding World Religions: An Interdisciplinary Approach*. Grand Rapids: Zondervan, 2011.

Hiebert, Paul. *Flaw of the Excluded Middle, Missiology* 10:1 (January 1982), 35-47.

http://mormon.org/jesus-christ/

http://quickfacts.census.gov/qfd/states/47000.html

http://www.adherents.com/Religions_By_Adherents.html

http://www.atheists.org/atheism

http://www.americancatholic.org/features/special/default.aspx?id=29

http://www.christianitytoday.com/ct/2011/july/indiagrassroots.html?start=2

http://www.4truth.net/fourtruthpbnew.aspx?pageid=8589952801

http://www.ijfm.org/PDFs_IJFM/11_2_PDFs/07_Love.pdf

http://www.pbs.org/edens/thailand/buddhism.htm

http://www.pioneermissions.org

http://www.watchtower.org/e/statistics/worldwide_report.htm

http://www.ywamcampaigns.org/Articles/1000067091/Impact_ World_Tour/Teaching/The_Engel_Scale.aspx

Johnson, Kevin. *Why Do Catholics Do That?* New York: Ballantine Books, 1994.

Martin, Walter Ralston. *The Kingdom of the Cults.* 3d ed. Hank H. Hanegraaff, gen. ed. Minneapolis: Bethany House, 1997.

Mandryk, Jason. *Operation World.* Colorado Springs: Biblica Publishing, 2010.

Mohler, R. Albert. *Atheism Remix: A Christian Confronts the New Atheists.* Wheaton, IL: Crossway, 2008.

Mead, Frank, Samuel Hill, and Craig Atwood. *Handbook of Denominations of the United States.* 12th ed. Nashville: Abingdon Press, 2005.

Muller, Roland. *Honor and Shame: Unlocking the Door.* N.p.: Xlibris, 2000.

Parshall, Phil. *The Cross and the Crescent: Understanding the Muslim Mind and Heart.* Wheaton, IL: Tyndale, 1989.

Pezzotta, Anthony. *Truth Encounter: Catholicism and the Holy Scriptures.* Richmond: FMB, 1996.

Roberts, Philip. *Mormonism Unmasked.* Nashville: Broadman & Holman, 1998.

Saal, William. *Reaching Muslims for Christ.* Chicago: Moody, 1991.

Stark, Rodney. *What Americans Really Believe.* Waco: Baylor University Press, 2008.

The Glorious Koran: A Bilingual Edition with English Translation, Introduction and Notes, translated by Marmaduke Pickthall. Albany: State University of New York Press, 1976.

Thirumalai, Madasamy. *Sharing Your Faith with a Buddhist.* Bloomington, MN: Bethany House, 2003.

_____. *Sharing Your Faith with a Hindu.* Minneapolis, MN: Bethany House, 2002.

Other Missions Titles from Hannibal Books

Sharing Your Faith with Muslims by Wade Akins. This book will teach you: who was Muhammad? is he the perfect model for the human race? how did he start the Muslim religion? what is the Koran? what are the keys to reading and understanding the Koran? what is in the Koran that causes violence? Learn what Islam teaches about God, the Bible, Jesus Christ, sin, salvation, afterlife, terrorism, women's rights, and more. Learn how to share your faith with Muslims in a practical way: practical tips, how God is using prayer, dreams, and visions, to reach Muslims, Islamic customs and things to avoid, how to start a conversation with Muslims, the Jesus approach, and evangelistic Bible studies for Muslims.

_____**Copies at $14.95=**_____

Be a 24/7 Christian by Wade Akins. Want to make Jesus truly the Lord of your life but don't know how? This renowned missionary evangelist/strategist tells how to live the adventure of being totally sold out to the Lord every moment of every day, every day of every year.

_____**Copies at $12.95=**_____

How to Be Spiritual without Being Weird by Christy Akins Brawner. Can you live a balanced, meaningful Christian life while still being "hip"? Contemporary young people who seek answers for crucial life questions need look no further than this sparkling, authentic Christian apologetic by Christy Brawner, daughter of *Sharing Your Faith with Muslims* author Wade Akins and wife of author Jeff Brawner. Christy Brawner shares personal experiences to demonstrate 12 core values people need to thrive in the modern world.

_____**Copies at $12.95=**_____

Add $4 shipping for first book, plus $1 for each additional book.
Shipping & handling _____
Texas residents add 8.25% sales tax _____
TOTAL ENCLOSED_____
check _____ or credit card # _____ exp. date_____
(Visa, MasterCard, Discover, American Express accepted)

Name _____

Address _____ Phone _____

City _____ State _____ Zip _____

See page 2 for address, phone number, email address, and website.

57332219R00126

Made in the USA
San Bernardino, CA
18 November 2017